SCOREBOARD SCORCHERS!

More Than 200 Red-Hot Basketball Plays To Help You Win More Games

Edited by Michael Podoll

Lessiter Publications, Inc. • Brookfield, WI

Publisher's Cataloging-in-Publication

(Provided by Quality Books, Inc.)

Scoreboard Scorchers: More Than 200 Red-Hot Basketball Plays To
   Help You Win More Games
   / edited by Michael Podoll. — 1st ed.

   p. cm.
   ISBN: 0-944079-44-X

   1. Basketball—Training. 2. Basketball—Coaching.
I. Podoll, Michael.

GV885.35.P76 2002   796.323'2
                             QBI02-200644

Cover and book design by Christopher Nielsen

International Standard Book Number: 0-944079-44-X

Published by Lessiter Publications, Inc.,
P.O. Box 624, Brookfield, WI 53008-0624.

For additional copies or information on other books or publications
offered by Lessiter Publications, write to the above address.

Telephone: (800) 645-8455 (US Only) or (262) 782-4480
Fax: (262) 782-1252 • E-Mail: info@lesspub.com
Web site: www.lesspub.com

Manufactured In The United States of America

FOREWORD

Add To Your Playbook...

IN THIS DAY of shared information and rapidly improving cost-effective technology, advanced scouting gets more thorough at all levels of competitive basketball — whether it be professional, college, high school, AAU and even higher-level youth leagues. With this growing level of sophisticated scouting and an overall increased knowledge of the game comes better defensive preparation and more complex, team-specific defensive schemes.

Staying One Step Ahead

No matter if you run a free-wheeling, up-tempo offense, prefer a motion attack or employ a more structured and controlled offensive style, you've got to find ways to counter the ever-evolving, tailor-made team defense of your upcoming opponents. That's why it is critical to keep your offense adaptable and to have a solid stable of set plays in your offensive arsenal for nearly every possible situation.

It's good to have a series of set plays that you can call upon during the course of a season that both complements your offensive philosophy and fits the talents of your players. There are many times during a game, when your players may lose focus and stop taking the type of quality shots you want. Set plays can help coaches overcome these frustrations, get players back on the right track and keep opponents honest.

Coaches can't be too controlling or run set plays exclusively, but the timing of running a good set play can help change the momentum of a game back in his or her team's favor.

Plenty To Choose From

Within the pages of *Scoreboard Scorchers!*, you'll find blackboard plays from successful coaches at all levels of competition. These hand-picked plays — organized and arranged in nine easy-to-use chapters covering the most critical game situations — will give your game plan a much-needed boost. If you can find just a few plays that complement your team's offensive philosophy and the talents of your players, it may make the difference in the handful of close ball games you'll find yourself in each season.

The difference between winning and losing can sometimes be marginal. Hopefully, the plays found in this book will arm you with the right offensive weaponry to put your offensive attack over the top and give your team a winning edge.

—Eric Musselman, Head Coach,
Golden State Warriors, Oakland, Calif.

CONTENTS

KEY TO DIAGRAMS

X Defensive Player or player in line during drill	⌁▶	Dribble
O Offensive Player	───▶	Cut
① Player with the ball	----▶	Pass
	⊢────	Screen/Trap

Chapter 1

SET PLAYS, OFFENSIVE INITIATORS

BASIC OFFENSE

Bill Agronin,
Head Womens Coach,
Niagara University, Niagara, N.Y.

This is a simple offensive set with three options. It provides player movement and a chance to get the ball into the lane for a layup or short jump shot.

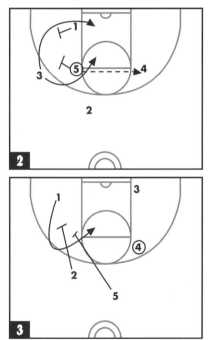

DIAGRAM 1: This is the initial set. 1 passes directly to 5, or to 2, who passes into 5. 1 goes backdoor off a back screen from 4. 1 cutting to the basket is the first option.

DIAGRAM 2: If 1 is not open, 5 passes to 4 stepping out. 5 and 1 set a double screen for 3. 3 either goes high or low, depending on the defense, and looks for the pass from 4.

DIAGRAM 3: If 3 does not receive the pass, 5 and 2 set staggered screens for 1, who curls into the middle.

1-4 LOW SERIES INTO THE FLEX

*Mack McCarthy, Former Head Mens Coach,
Virginia Commonwealth University,
Richmond, Va.*

DIAGRAM 1: From a 1-4 low set, 1 dribbles right and reverses a pass to 5 popping to the weak-side elbow. 4 steps out and sets a screen for 2, who reads the screen and cuts either above or below the screen to the opposite block.

DIAGRAM 2: 1 fades to the corner, while 4 pops up top to receive a pass from 5. 2 sets a screen for 3 who breaks to the opposite low block. 5 throws a pass to 4. 4 now has the option to shoot, hit 3 in the low post or to swing the ball to 1 in the corner for a quick 3-pointer. If there's no scoring opportunity, you can now run your continuity/flex offense.

DIAGRAM 3: Backcut Option. 1 dribbles right. 5 pops to the top, but then quickly backcuts toward the basket. 1 can look to hit 5 going to the hoop. 3 quickly fills the open spot vacated by 5. If 5 doesn't receive the ball on the backcut, he or she should refill 3's spot in the weak-side corner.

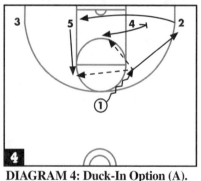

DIAGRAM 4: Duck-In Option (A). If 4's defender helps out too much on 2's cut, then 4 may duck in and look for a quick pass for a post-up opportunity in the middle, near the dotted line. After the ball is reversed, 1 fades to the corner.

DIAGRAM 5: Duck-In Option (B). 5 refills 1's spot with a few hard dribbles to the right. 2 breaks up to the weak-side elbow, while 4 slides back down to the low post. 5 reverses to 2 and you run continuity.

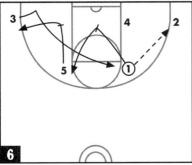

DIAGRAM 6: Corner Option. If the ball is passed into the corner (1 to 2), both 1 and 5 will set staggered screens for the opposite corner. 3 cuts off the staggered screens and breaks to the middle looking for a pass from 2 or refilling at the strong-side elbow. After screening, 1 refills to the weak-side guard spot and 5 fades to the weak-side corner.

DIAGRAM 7: Bump Option (A). After the ball is reversed (see Diagram 1), if 2's defender jumps over 4's screen, 2 may yell "Bump!" and replace to his or her original corner. 4 turns and re-screens 2's defender. 5 throws a diagonal pass to 2.

DIAGRAM 8: Bump Option (B). After the diagonal pass is thrown to 2, 5 and 1 will set a staggered screen for 3. 3 cuts to the strong-side guard spot and looks for a pass from 2 for a quick shot. 1 refills to the weak-side elbow and 5 into the weak-side corner.

LOW-POST DOUBLE-STACK WITH COUNTERS

John Stroia, Assistant Mens Coach,
Weber State University,
Ogden, Utah

1

DIAGRAM 1: 2 and 4 form a stack on the left-side low-block, while 3 and 5 stack on the right-side low block. 1 has the ball on top and begins the action by dribbling left.

2 curls around 4 and continues to the other side. 3 curls around 5 and comes to the top to receive any potential ball reversal.

2

DIAGRAM 2: 1 has the option to enter the ball in to 4 on the block for a post-up opportunity.

DIAGRAM 3: A second option is to have 1 throw a pass to 3, with 3 swinging the ball quickly over to 2 on the opposite side. 2 can either shoot or dump it in to 5 on the low block.

3

4

DIAGRAM 4: Counter-Cross Option. A counter to the original action, this play starts with 2 and 3 crossing underneath the basket. One of them screens for the other (in this diagram, 2 screens for 3). Both players come off screens by the top player in the stack (4 and 5) and roll to the wing areas behind the 3-point line.

1 can pass to either player for a quick jump shot.

DIAGRAM 5: 4 and 5 set cross-screens for one another in the lane and post up on their respective low block.

DIAGRAM 6: Counter 2. In this counter, have your best shooter (in this diagram, player 2) come off a double

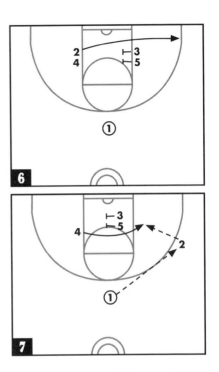

screen from 3 and 5, popping out to the right corner.

DIAGRAM 7: 3 and 5 roll back into the lane and set a double screen for 4, who crosses through the lane and posts up on the opposite low block. 1 passes to 2, who either shoots or dumps it in to 4 in the low post.

SCREEN AND PICK

Marc Comstock,
Emporia State University,
Emporia, Kan.

DIAGRAM 1: 5 sets a ball screen for 1 who dribbles left and immediately looks for 5 coming off 2's screen and rolling to the hoop for a lob pass. 4 sets a down screen for 3. After the screen,

4 curls into post up position. 1 can pass to 3 if a 3-point shot is wide open.

DIAGRAM 2: If 3 is not open, 1 passes to 2 popping out to the top of the key. 2 dribbles right and looks to 5 posting up on the block.

COMBO PLAYS FOR BEST SHOOTER

Dick Manzo,
Southern Regional High School,
Manahawkin, N.J.

These set plays are designed to get your best shooter the ball in various situations.

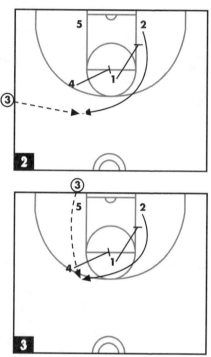

DIAGRAM 1: From Floor. 1 starts the play by passing to 3 on the wing. 1 and 4 cut down and set a double screen for 2. 2 cuts off the screens for an open shot at the top of the key.

DIAGRAM 2: From Sideline. Use the same double screen by 1 and 4 to set up an open look for 2 off the inbounds pass.

DIAGRAM 3: From Endline. Again, 1 and 4 set a double screen to get 2 an open shot. 2 may have to cut farther out to the wing to get open on this play.

"EAGLE"

John Kimble, Former Head Coach,
Crestview High SChool,
Crestview, Fla.

DIAGRAM 1: 1 has the ball up top, while 3 and 5 set in a stack at the left elbow. 2 and 4 line up in a stack on the right low block. 1 draws the defense with a dribble entry to the middle for a few steps, then dribbles to the right corner.

2 V-cuts to the basket, then pops out to the ball-side corner, while 4 breaks to mid-post, then rolls to the basket. 5 replaces 1 at the top of the key and 3 sprints to the weak-side wing area.

1 looks to hit either 4 in the mid post or rolling to the basket or passes to 2 in the corner for a quick jump shot.

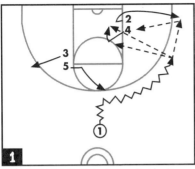

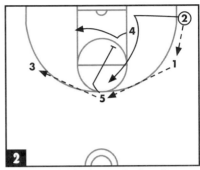

DIAGRAM 2: If the jump shot isn't there, 2 reverses the ball back to 1 who quickly passes to 5. 5 swings the ball to 3.

After swinging the ball to 3, 5 breaks to the basket and sets a mid-lane screen for 4, who uses the screen and rolls to the ball-side block. 2 breaks to the basket on the baseline then pops and replaces 5 at the top of the key.

3 can either shoot a quick, open 3-pointer or throw an entry pass to 4 in the low post for a scoring opportunity.

EASY BUCKET FOR POST PLAYER

Dale Herl,
Jetmore High School,
Jetmore, Kan.

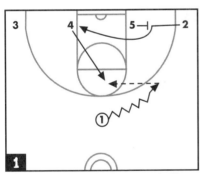

DIAGRAM 1: 1 comes across half court and declares a direction with the dribble. The opposite post player (4) flashes to the middle of the lane at the free-throw line.

On the pass from 1 to 4, 2 flex cuts off a screen from 5. 5 shouldn't have to move at all for this screen.

DIAGRAM 2: The pass from 4 to 2 is the first option. After setting the screen for 2, 5 steps into the lane and looks for a pass from 4.

BOX SPECIAL

Nathan Livesay, Head Coach,
A.C. Flora High School,
Columbia, S.C.

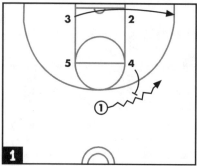

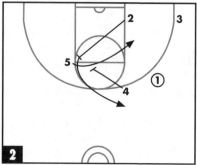

DIAGRAM 1: This play is run out of a box set and uses screen-the-screener action to get a shot in the post or on the perimeter. Players set up in a box set with 4 and 5 at the elbows, with 2 and 3 at each low-post block. 1 brings the ball upcourt. 4 pops up and sets an up screen for 1 who uses the screen and dribbles to the right. 3 cuts across the lane to the ball side and sets up behind the 3-point line.

DIAGRAM 2: 2 breaks up to the opposite elbow and sets a screen for 5 who rolls to the opposite low-post block. 4 screens the screener and 2 breaks to the top of the 3-point circle. 1 can feed 5 in the post, 2 for a quick jump shot or hit 3 in the corner. If the pass goes to 3, he or she can either shoot the three or hit 5 in the post.

BOSTON CELTICS "POWER" SERIES

Mark Starns,
Former Video Coordinator,
Boston Celtics, Boston, Mass.

"POWER"

DIAGRAM 1: 1 drives off an angle pick-and-roll set by 4. 4 steps out after screening for 1. 5 ducks into the lane hard.
DIAGRAM 2: 1 has the option to drive to the basket, or pass to 4 or 5.

"POWER UP"

DIAGRAM 3: 1 drives off an angle screen from 5. 5 dives hard into the lane as soon as 1 goes by. 4 cuts hard to replace 5 at the top.

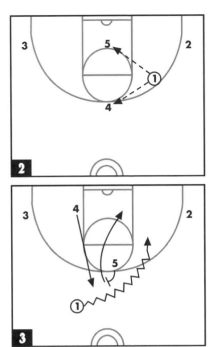

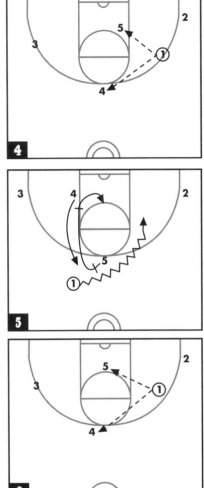

DIAGRAM 4: 1 can pass to 4 or 5.

"POWER DOWN"

DIAGRAM 5: 5 sets an angle pick-and-roll screen for 1. 1 penetrates as far as possible. As 1 goes by, 5 rolls to set a downscreen for 4. 4 replaces 5. 5 ducks into the lane.

DIAGRAM 6: 1 can drive to the basket or pass to either 4 or 5.

> *"Give me twelve players that want to win and they will find a way to win."*
>
> —Red Auerbach

"NOTRE DAME"

Mike Faletti, Head Coach,
Michigan Mustangs AAU,
Farmington Hills, Mich.

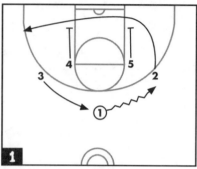

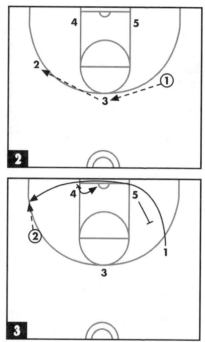

DIAGRAM 1: 1 dribbles to the right wing and waves 2 to cut toward the basket and along the baseline to the opposite corner. 4 and 5 set screens for 2 cutting along the baseline. 3 replaces 1 at the top of the key. After setting the screens, 4 and 5 post up inside on each low block.

DIAGRAM 2: 1 throws a pass to 3, who quickly reverses the ball to 2 on the opposite side, for an open jump shot. If the shot isn't there, 2 can look to quickly dump it down to 4 in the low post.

DIAGRAM 3: If neither scoring option is there, then 4 and 5 should set staggered screens along the baseline for 1 who cuts off the screens and breaks to the ball-side corner. 2 hits 1 for a quick jump shot or looks for 4 rolling to the basket.

"Basketball is like a really fast-paced game of chess, where every move has its benefits and repercussions."

—Bill Walton

BOX TO POWER (VS. MAN)

Nate Webber, Head Boys Coach,
Nottingham High School,
Trenton, N.J.

DIAGRAM 1: Set up in a box set with both post players at the elbows and 2 and 3 lined up on each low block. 1 has the ball at the top and initiates the action by dribbling to the right.

3 sets a cross screen for 2 who uses the screen and breaks along the baseline toward the ball side. 4 and 5 set a downscreen in the middle of the lane for 3 who breaks to the top of the key after setting the screen for 2.

DIAGRAM 2: 4 and 5 both break to the weak-side low block and set a double screen for 2 who reverses back along the baseline to the weak-side

corner. 1 passes to 3 who quickly looks to hit 2 coming off the double screen.

DIAGRAM 3: If 2 isn't open for a shot, then 3 keeps the ball and makes a dribble entry to the left side of the floor. 2 and 4 break to the opposite side of the floor and 1 swings to the short corner on the weak side.

DIAGRAM 4: 3 dribbles the ball back out to the top of the key, while 2 and 1 break across the middle and set a double screen for 5. 5 pops out behind the 3-point line and receives a pass from 3 and looks to shoot a quick 3-pointer.

BACKDOOR LOB

Brad Duncan,
Fox High School,
Arnold, Mo.

DIAGRAM 1: The play starts with a 1-2-2 set. (1 is the point. 2 and 3 are the wings. 4 and 5 are the post.) 1 passes to either wing. The opposite wing cuts through to the corner off the screen at the block. The post player on the ball side immediately posts hard and must draw attention from the defense.

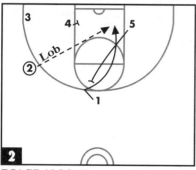

DIAGRAM 2: The opposite post player sets a back pick for 1. 1 cuts off of the back pick and goes backdoor for the lob. 1 must set the pick up by waiting for the back pick. This play works if: **A.** The ball-side post player posts hard and draws the defender away from help-side defense. **B.** 1 waits for the back pick and draws the defender

in the opposite direction of where the pick is coming.

DIAGRAM 3: Alternate Play A.
Starts out in a 1-2-2 set (same positions). 1 passes to either wing. Opposite wing cuts through to the corner off of the screen at the block. The post player on the ball side immediately posts up hard and must draw attention from the defense as a threat.

DIAGRAM 4: The opposite post player sets a back pick for 1. 1 cuts off the back pick and floats to the opposite wing looking for the skip pass and a shot. 2 either looks to throw a lob to 4 in the post or throws a skip pass to 1 on the opposite wing.

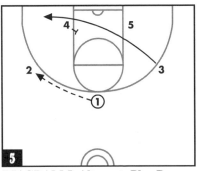

DIAGRAM 5: Alternate Play B.
Starts out in a 1-2-2 set (same positions). 1 passes to either wing. Opposite wing cuts through to the corner off the screen at the block. The post player on the ball side immediately posts up hard and must draw attention from the defense as a threat.

DIAGRAM 6: The opposite post player sets a back pick for 1, but this time, 1 cuts to the basket as if to get the lob, but then V-cuts out to the wing at the free-throw line extended.

DIAGRAM 7: 4 sets a screen for 3 who breaks toward the basket along the baseline. 2 passes to 5 who quickly skip passes to 1. 1 looks for 3 in the post.

PICK AND PASS TO CUTTER

Shawn Huse,
Montana Tech,
Butte, Mont.

DIAGRAM 1: 1 dribbles to the left and stops. After picking up the dribble, 1 must turn and do a ball-fake pass to jab-stepping 2. 2 jab steps to the top then turns and cuts to the basket. 1 throws a bounce pass for a backdoor layup to 2. 3 and 4 set a double screen for 5 cutting across the lane. If the backdoor cut to 2 is not open, 1 looks for 5 coming off the screen.

"MICHIGAN STATE" SPECIAL (VS. ZONE OR MAN)

Steve Pappas, Head Boys Coach,
Deerfield High School,
Deerfield, Ill.

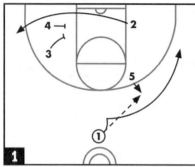

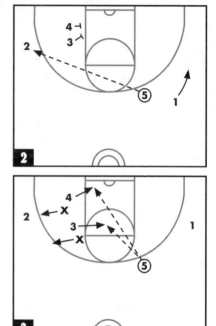

DIAGRAM 1: Player 1 passes to 5 and follows the pass, cutting to the wing area. 4 and 3 set a double screen and 2 cuts from the ball-side low block and curls around the screens to the off-side 3-point area.

DIAGRAM 2: 4 and 3 maintain the screens. 5 throws a skip pass to 2 for a 3-pointer.

DIAGRAM 3: When the defenders jump out to defend against 2 shooting a 3-pointer or cheat off the screen to prevent the pass, the screeners slip into the open areas. 5 reads the action, fakes a skip pass to 2 and passes to the open player for the best shot possible.

"The best teams have chemistry.
They communicate with each other and they
sacrifice personal glory for a common goal."

—Dave DeBusschere

BACKDOOR TRIANGLE

John Rysewyk,
Oliver Springs High School,
Oliver Springs, Tenn.

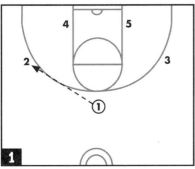

DIAGRAM 1: Initial Set. 1 passes to 2.

DIAGRAM 2: 1 follows the pass and sets an on-the-ball screen for 2. 4 pops up to the ball-side elbow.

DIAGRAM 3: 1 and 4 set staggered screens for 2, who tries to lose his or her

defender off the screen and dribbles to the middle of the floor and toward the basket for a few steps. This hopefully will draw a defender or two, as they step over trying to stop 2's penetration.

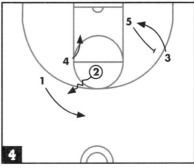

DIAGRAM 4: 5 pops out and sets a screen for 3 who breaks hard toward the basket. 2 pulls the ball back out top with a few dribbles, while 1 goes to the top of the key. 4 rolls toward the basket and posts up.

DIAGRAM 5: 2 can shoot a short jumper from the foul line, hit 3 on the backdoor cut, dump the ball in to 4 in the low post or kick it back out to 1 on top to re-start the offense.

"HORNS"

Trevor Gleeson, Assistant Coach,
Sioux Falls Sky Force, CBA,
Sioux Falls, S.D.

The object of this play is to get the ball into the post or to your best offensive player in the post.

If there is a weak defender or if a certain player is in foul trouble, we'll call this play.

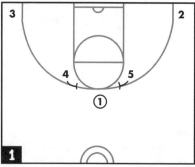

DIAGRAM 1: 1 has the ball at the top of the key. 4 and 5 are positioned at the top near the 3-point circle. 2 and 3 are in the corners. 4 and 5 begin by setting a double screen for the ball handler.

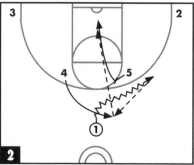

DIAGRAM 2: 1 comes off the double screen and and dribbles right. After setting the screen, 5 rolls toward the basket. 4 steps out to the top of the key. 1 looks to throw a lob pass to 5 or reverses the ball back to 4.

DIAGRAM 3: "Horns" Counter Play 1. 4 also looks to lob the ball into the post. If that option isn't open, he or she should swing the ball to 3 in the corner. 3 looks to throw the ball inside to 5. 5 should try to keep the defender on his or her back while rolling to face 3's side.

DIAGRAM 4: "Horns" Counter Play 2. If 4 is denied the ball at the top of the key, 1 can pass to 3 in the opposite corner. 5 tries to seal the defender in the post.

POST PLAY

Raymond Townsend, Head Mens Coach,
Menlo College,
Atherton, Calif.

DIAGRAM 1: 1 starts to dribble toward 5, then crosses over to the other side of the floor. 2 and 3 cross to clear out the middle. 4 and 3 then screen across the lane for 5. 5 establishes position on the post box and looks for a pass from 1.

DIAGRAM 2: If 5 is not open on the immediate look, 5 comes up the lane as 1 reverses the ball to the weak side, 1 to 3 to 4. After 2 sets a downscreen for 4, 2 sprints up the lane to set a "little-on-big" screen for 5. 4 receives the swing pass and looks inside for 5.

"PUSHDOWN" — BACKCUT FOR A LAYUP

Kevin Wenzel,
West Central High School,
Francesville, Ind.

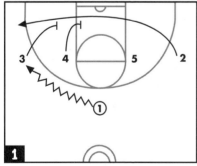

DIAGRAM 1: 3 and 4 set a staggered screen for 2. 1 dribbles toward 2 who is coming off the double screen.

DIAGRAM 2: 5 steps out and calls for the ball, then backcuts toward the hoop. 1 fakes a pass to 2 and then hits 5 on the backcut for a layup.

STAGGERED HI-LOW

Mack McCarthy, Former Head Mens Coach,
Virginia Commonwealth University,
Richmond, Va.

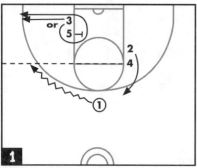

DIAGRAM 1: To Left Side. 3 and 5 stack on the low block on the left side, while 2 and 4 set up a double-stack on the right elbow. 1 dribbles left, staying above the free-throw-line extended.

3 pops out to the corner and 5 posts. If 3 is fronted, 5 sets a screen and 3 will curl around the screen and break to the corner. When 1 gets to the free-throw-line-extended area, 2 pops out behind the 3-point line at the top.

DIAGRAM 2: 4 steps out and sets a back screen for 2, who rolls around the screen and breaks hard toward the bas-

ket. 1 looks to hit 2 with a lob pass on the backdoor cut to the basket.

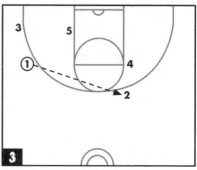

DIAGRAM 3: Another option can be for 1 to immediately pass to 2 for a quick 3-point shot.

DIAGRAM 4: To The Right Side. When 1 dribbles right and crosses the lane-line extended, 2 pops out wide behind 1, 3 cuts across to the strong-side corner, 4 slides down the lane to the low post and 5 flashes hard to the strong-side high post.

OVERLOAD OFFENSE

Rick Berger,
Former Head Womens Coach
Westfield State College, Westfield, Mass.

DIAGRAM 1: 1 enters to 2 who faces the hoop and steps up. 2 looks for 5 posting up or 4 flashing high. If 4 or 5 are not open, pass to 3 in the corner.

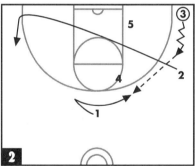

DIAGRAM 2: When 3 receives the ball in the corner, the player again looks for 5, then 4. After passing to 3, 2 goes through to the opposite wing. If there is no entry available, 3 dribbles to the wing and reverses the ball to 1.

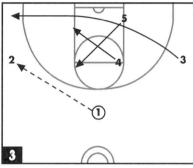

DIAGRAM 3: 1 reverses ball to 2. 4 and 5 cross. 3 goes to the opposite corner while 2 looks for 4 low then 5 high.

DIAGRAM 4: If 4 and 5 are not open, 2 enters the ball to 3 and cuts through. Continue in the same pattern.

"They say good things come to those who wait. I believe good things come to those who work."

—*Wilt Chamberlain*

"PORTLAND"

Andy Manning, Former Coach,
Jacksonville University,
Jacksonville, Fla.

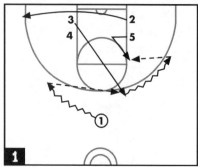

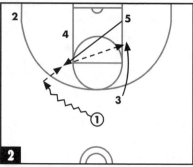

DIAGRAM 1: From a low double-stack formation, 1 has the ball on top and dribbles to the left. 2 crosses along the baseline and cuts to the ball-side corner. 3 breaks from the ball-side low block to the top of the key. 5 cuts into the lane, but then V-cuts to the weak-side elbow.

1 passes to 3, who takes a few hard dribbles to the right and passes to 5 at the elbow for a short jump shot.

DIAGRAM 2: If 3's defender is over-playing, then 5 must automatically come up to the ball-side elbow. 1 dribbles left and passes to 5 at the elbow. 5 looks for 3 on the backcut to the basket for a lob pass.

If 3 isn't open, you are now in perfect position to transition into your 3-out, 2-in motion offense.

"SPECIAL"

Bill Agronin, Head Womens Coach,
Niagara University,
Niagara, N.Y.

DIAGRAM 1: 1 dribbles toward the wing area. 5 sets a quick back screen for 2. 2 uses the screen and breaks to the block. 3 lines up behind the 3-point line in the wing area, while 4 posts up on the weak-side block

DIAGRAM 2: After 2 gets to the block, 5 sets another screen for 2 who comes off the screen looking for the shot. 4 breaks just above the free-throw

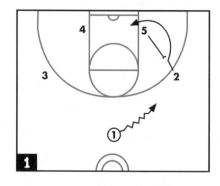

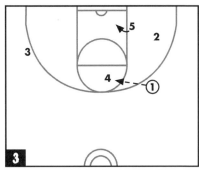

line looking for a pass from 1. If 2 isn't open for a quick shot, then 1 passes to 4.

DIAGRAM 3: After 4 gets the pass from 1, then 5 should curl and roll to the basket. 4 looks for an open jump shot or passes to 5 if 5 has sealed the defender and has a good look.

"DIVE"

Tubby Smith, Head Mens Coach,
University of Kentucky,
Lexington, Ky.

DIAGRAM 1: Initial set. 1 has the ball to the side. 5 lines up on the ball-side block, 2 sets up in the ball-side corner, 4 sets at the top of the key and 3 goes to the weak-side wing area behind the 3-point line.

1 dribbles left to the top of the key. 5 breaks across the lane and sets a screen for 3. 4 dives hard to the basket.

1 passes to 3. 3 has the go-ahead to shoot a quick three-pointer if open. If 3 isn't open, 3 and 5 should run a pick-and-roll.

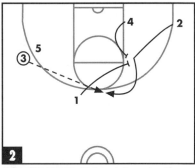

DIAGRAM 2: If the pick-and-roll isn't open, 1 and 4 set a double screen near the elbow and 2 comes off the screen and receives a pass from 3. 2 looks for a quick 3-point shot.

PHANTOM

Joseph F. Nasta,
Monmouth Power AAU
Manalapan, N.J.

DIAGRAM 1: This play is used against a team that can dominate low-post play with skill and height. 3 and 2 set up as wide. 1 has the ball on top.

4 and 5 leave their positions after establishing low-post positions and quickly screen for 3 and 2 on top.

DIAGRAM 2: 1 passes to 3 and follows the pass and continues to run baseline. This occupies the low-post defenders. Speed is essential. The screener, after setting the screen, moves back to prepare for the rebound. 3 must immediately react to the screen by taking a jump shot or penetrating.

Even in a man-to-man defense, the low defenders will only follow the screeners halfway. That is where the wide set up comes into play. If 3 shoots or penetrates immediately, the low defender is momentarily caught flat-footed.

"BEAR"

John Kimble, Former Head Coach,
Crestview High School,
Crestview, Fla.

DIAGRAM 1: 1 has the ball out top with 3 and 5 in a double stack on the left elbow, while 2 and 4 line up in a double stack on the right low block.

5 pops out and sets a ball screen for 1 who makes a dribble entry to the left side of the floor. 3 cuts to the weak-side corner.

DIAGRAM 2: 2 breaks to the weak-side wing area and 4 flashes to the

2

middle of the lane. 1 passes to 5 at the top of the key.

3

DIAGRAM 3: 5 can hit 4 in the lane for a post-up opportunity in the middle or can pass to 2 on the wing and look for a return pass on his or her cut to the basket.

4

DIAGRAM 4: Another option can be for 5 to pass to 2 and then screen away for 1 who breaks to the top of the key. 2 swings the ball to 3 in the corner.

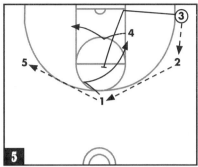

5

DIAGRAM 5: 3 kicks the ball back out to 2. After making the pass, 3 cuts hard along the baseline toward the basket, then breaks up toward the foul line and sets a screen for 1. 2 passes to 1, who swings the ball to 5 popping out behind the 3-point line. 1 uses 3's screen and cuts to the basket. 4 rolls across the lane and posts up on the low block.

6

DIAGRAM 6: 5 looks to hit 4 in the low post. If 4 isn't open, 5 kicks it back out top to 3. On the pass, 1 rolls across the lane and screens for 4, who uses the screen and flashes to the other side of the lane and posts up. The ball rotation and motion continues until an open shot becomes available.

BASIC POWER SET

Rick Berger, Former Womens Head Coach,
Westfield State College,
Westfield, Mass.

DIAGRAM 1: 1 starts with the ball out top, while 2 and 3 line up wide on the wings. 4 and 5 line up on each block.

DIAGRAM 2: 2 V-cuts to the basket and pops out behind the 3-point line. 1 passes to 2, then breaks down the lane and sets a downscreen for 4, who cuts to the free-throw line. 1 takes two hard dribbles into the corner.

DIAGRAM 3: 3 sets a downscreen for 1 at the weak-side low block. 2 passes to 4 who quickly reverses the ball to 1 popping behind the 3-point line.

DIAGRAM 4: 4 sets a downscreen for 5 who curls around the screen and goes to the top of the key. 2 "screens-the-screener" for 4 who breaks around the

screen and releases behind the 3-point line on the weak side. 1 takes two hard dribbles into the corner.

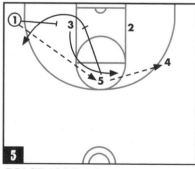

DIAGRAM 5: 1 throws a pass to 5 who swings the ball over to 4. After swinging the ball, 5 breaks down the

lane and sets a screen for 3. 3 breaks from the ball-side block, comes around the screen and sets up at the elbow toward 4's side of the floor. 1 breaks in and sets a screen for 5 who curls around the screen and sets up behind

the 3-point line on the weak side.

4 can shoot a 3-pointer, throw it down to 2 in the low block or hit 3 at the elbow. 3 can either shoot a jump shot or swing the ball to 5 on the weak side and the motion would continue.

"CHICAGO" (INTO FLEX OFFENSE)

Duane Sigsbury,
Woburn High School,
Woburn, Mass.

This is an offensive set that gives you four great looks to score. The set ends up in the flex offense. It's a good way to disguise your flex offense.

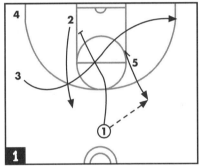

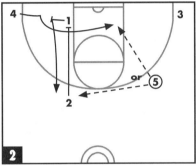

DIAGRAM 1: Phase 1. 5 V-cuts to get open. 1 passes to 5 and cuts to the weak-side block and sets a screen for 2, who uses the screen and pops up to the top of the key. 5 looks to pass to 3 on a shuffle cut (first scoring option). If 3 isn't open, 5 looks for 2 for a quick 3-pointer (second scoring option).
DIAGRAM 2: Phase 2. 1 sets a screen for 4 who makes a flex cut and goes through the lane. 5 looks for 4 on the flex cut (third scoring option). 2 breaks and sets a downscreen for 1, who pops back out to the top. 5 looks

for 1 for a quick 3-pointer (fourth scoring option).

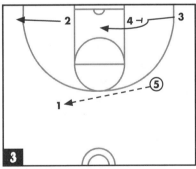

DIAGRAM 3: Flex Offense. If none of the scoring options are open, your players are now set up in position for the flex offense and they can begin the flex motion.

"DOUBLE" FROM 1-2-2 SET

Greg Fortner,
Fox High School,
Arnold, Mo.

DIAGRAM 1: 1 passes to 2 on the wing and sets a downscreen for 5 near the block. 5 pops to the top of the key and 1 clears to the wing.

DIAGRAM 2: 2 reverses the ball to 5 at the top. As soon as 2 releases the ball, 3 moves across the lane and sets a screen for 2. 4 moves up to set a screen for 2.

DIAGRAM 3: 5 reverses the ball to 1 on the wing. As soon as 5 releases the ball, 2 breaks either high or low off the double screen. If 2 doesn't receive the ball, he or she should post up on the block.

DIAGRAM 4: If 2 doesn't receive the ball, 3 and 5 set a staggered double screen for 4. 1 passes to 4. 2 cuts to the block and slips into rebounding position on any shot.

3-2 DOUBLE POST SCREEN, CURL

Joshua Venegas,
Belmont, Calif.

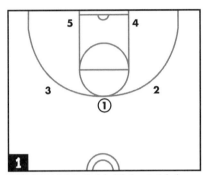

DIAGRAM 1: 3-2 initial set. 1 brings the ball down the middle of the floor to the top of the key. 1 signals to indicate which way the play will go.

DIAGRAM 2: If the play is called for 2, 2 cuts toward the basket and curls off the double screen set by 4 and 5. 1 passes to 3 who passes to 2 coming off the screens. 2 looks for the 3-point shot or a entry pass to 5 posting on the low block.

DIAGRAM 3: This is the same play with 3 going to the other side.

DIAGRAM 4: The 4 or 5 option coming out of the same set. After you've run this play a few times the defense will be ready for it. Mix it up by having 2 break toward the basket, the same as with the previous set, but this time 2 sets a screen for 5 who either curls around 4's screen or breaks to the corner for a jump shot. This can also be run to the other side with 3 screening and 4 coming off the screens.

"TWO"

Greg Zeller,
Concord High School,
Concord, Mich.

We call this play "Two" because the first option is for 2 to get a jump shot. However, there are other options.

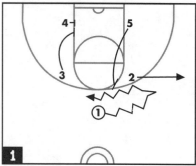

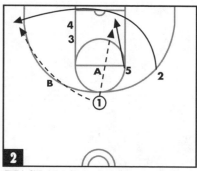

DIAGRAM 1: 1 dribbles toward 2 as 5 comes to the ball-side elbow. 3 and 4 set up a double screen on the weak side. 1 reverses the dribble and comes off a screen from 5.

DIAGRAM 2: As 1 dribbles over the screen, 2 runs baseline off the double screen and 5 rolls to the basket. 1 can either pass to 5 rolling to the basket (first option) or pass to 2 in the corner (second option).

After you've run this play a few times, 2's defender will work extra hard to get through the double screen. 2 can stop for a quick, short lob from 1.

"GATOR"

Ricky Norris,
Harriman High School,
Harriman, Tenn.

DIAGRAM 1: Both post players set a high screen for 1 who dribbles to the right side of the floor. After setting the screen, 4 rolls toward the basket. 1 and 4 can look for a quick screen-and-roll.
DIAGRAM 2: 1 dribbles deep into the corner and hands the ball off to 2 who dribbles back out toward the top. 5 starts to set up a ball screen near the top by the ball-side elbow.

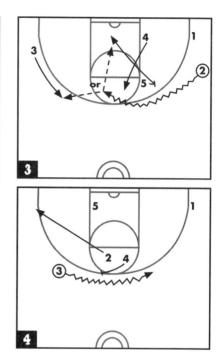

DIAGRAM 3: 2 dribbles across the top and off 5's screen. After setting the screen, 5 rolls toward the basket. 2 looks for 5 for a quick screen-and-roll play. 3 breaks to the top and receives a pass from 2.

DIAGRAM 4: 2 breaks to the corner. 5 floats near the basket. 4 sets a screen for 3 who dribbles across the top and the weave action continues.

DOUBLE STACK

Mack McCarthy, Former Head Coach,
Virginia Commonwealth University,
Richmond, Va.

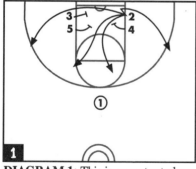

Set up a double stack on each side of the low block with 3 and 5 on one side and 2 and 4 on the other low block. 1 has the ball up top.

1 calls out a player's name and everyone screens for that player (in this case 2). The player comes off one of the screens, gets a pass from 1 and works for a good shot.

The player with the ball should also look for one of the screeners rolling to the basket. There may be a mix-up on a defensive switch and someone may be open for a good look.

DIAGRAM 1: This is a great set play to get the ball to a particular player for a scoring opportunity or isolation on one side of the floor.

"THUMBS UP"

Mike Faletti,
Michigan Mustangs AAU,
Farmington Hills, Mich.

DIAGRAM 1: 1 brings the ball up and passes to 5 at the right elbow. 2 sets a screen for 4 who breaks to the low post on the right side. If 4 is open early while coming off 2's screen, then 5 should hit 4 for a quick layup.

DIAGRAM 2: If 4 isn't open, 5 takes a few dribbles toward 1 near the center of the foul line, looking for a quick handoff if possible. If no handoff can be made, 1 fades into the right corner behind the 3-point line.

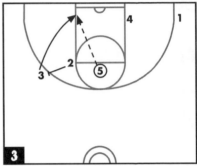

DIAGRAM 3: 2 sets a back screen for 3 who comes hard off the screen and breaks toward the basket. 1 looks to hit 3 cutting to the basket for a quick layup or 8- to 10-foot jump shot.

DIAGRAM 4: If that option isn't open, 5 passes to 2 for a jump shot. If 2 can't get a good, open shot off, then he or she brings the ball back up top to call another player or restart the "thumbs-up" motion.

POST ISOLATION PLAY

Marty Gaughan, Head Boys Coach,
Benet Academy,
Lisle, Ill.

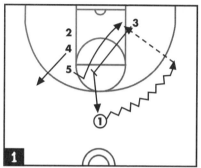

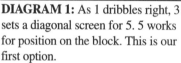

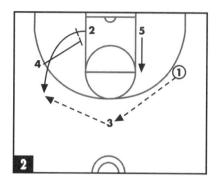

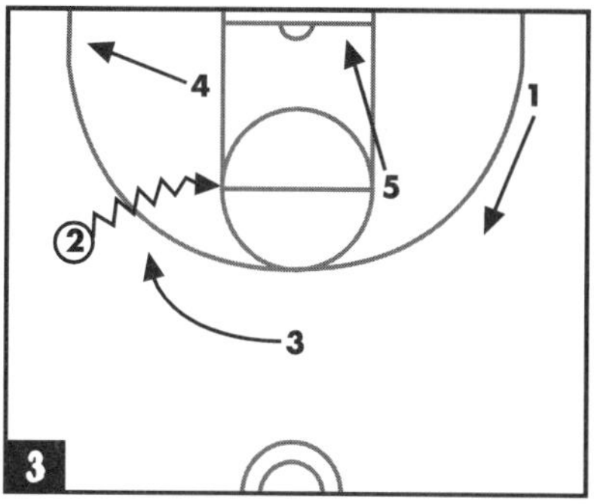

DIAGRAM 1: As 1 dribbles right, 3 sets a diagonal screen for 5. 5 works for position on the block. This is our first option.

DIAGRAM 2: If 5 can't establish position, 1 reverse passes to 3. On the ball reversal, 4 downscreens for 2 and 5 slides up the lane. 3 passes to 2.

DIAGRAM 3: The first option is for 2 to feed the ball to 4 in the post. If the defense drops, 2 dribbles into the gap and looks to draw an extra defender, so that he or she can hit the most open player for the spot-up jumper.

> *"Talent wins games, but teamwork and intelligence wins championships."*
>
> —*Michael Jordan*

DOUBLE EAGLE

Brian McCormick, Coach And Director,
High Five Hoops School,
Sacramento, Calif.

DIAGRAM 1: Play is initiated with the point guard (1) dribbling near the 3-point line, free-throw line extended. 5 sets a high pick-and-roll with the ball handler dribbling toward the middle of the floor, either looking for the shot or a pass to the cutter rolling to the basket.

As the screen is being set, 3 clears out, rubbing off a staggered screen on the weak side looking for a shot. If 3 gets the ball but not the shot, 4 seals the defender and looks for a post entry.

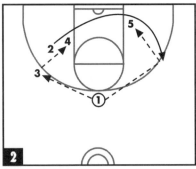

DIAGRAM 2: As 3 rubs off 2's shoulders, 2 runs the baseline rubbing the defender off screens set by 4 and 5 and looks for a shot. If 2 gets the ball and doesn't have an open shot, then 5 seals the defender and looks for a post-entry pass. Or 2 can hit 4 flashing to the high post for a foul-line jumper.

DIAGRAM 3: After 2 uses a screen, 4 flashes to the ball and the high post, clearing out the weak side for 3 to go backdoor. If 4 gets the ball, he or she shoots, looks immediately for the backdoor cut by 3 or for a high-low entry with 5, who seals the defender.

DIAGRAM 4: If the ball gets kicked back to 2, he or she first looks to shoot. 4 and 1 set a double screen for 3, who pops to the foul line and looks for a pass from 2 and the open shot.

5-WIDE BREAKDOWN

Mack McCarthy, Former Head Coach,
Virginia Commonwealth University,
Richmond, Va.

DIAGRAM 1: 1 has the ball up top. 5 and 4 set up wide behind the 3-point line in each corner, while 2 and 3 line up wide behind the 3-point line at the free-throw line extended on each side of the floor.

1 passes to 2, then breaks down hard to the middle of the lane and sets a screen for 3, who reads the defense and cuts either over or under the screen and sets up on the strong-side low-block

area. 5 replaces 3 wide on the weak-side wing area. After setting the screen down low, 1 pops back out to the top of the key.

DIAGRAM 2: 2 passes to 1 who quickly swings the ball to 5. 3 sets a back pick for 2, who uses 3's screen and cuts to the basket and into the corner on 5's side of the floor. 3 replaces 2 wide. 5 can shoot, hit 1 in the corner for a 3-pointer or run continuity.

"My definition of discipline is as follows:
(1) Do what has to be done, when it has to
be done, as well as it can be done, and
(2) Do it that way all the time."

—Bobby Knight

Chapter 2

BASELINE, UNDER-THE-BASKET INBOUNDS PLAYS

"FIVE" BASELINE OUT-OF-BOUNDS

Kimberly Jenkins,
Valley Springs High School,
Valley Springs, Ark.

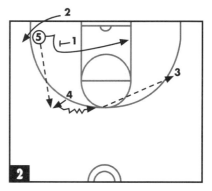

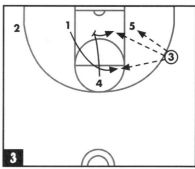

DIAGRAM 1: Player 2 takes the ball out. 1 sets a screen for 5 coming across to the ball-side corner. 4 sets a back screen for 3, who comes off the screen and either tries to sneak toward the basket or pops to the opposite wing area. 1 passes to 5.

DIAGRAM 2: 5 passes to 4. 1 sets a screen for 5, who comes hard off the screen and breaks to the opposite block. 4 dribbles right and passes to 3 at the wing. 2 floats behind the 3-point line on the weak side.

DIAGRAM 3: 4 sets a downscreen for 1 who pops to the free-throw line. After setting the screen, 4 rolls toward the basket. 3 can pass to 5 who's posting on the block, 4 rolling to the basket or to 1. If the pass goes to 1, 1 can shoot or look for 4.

"FLEX" UNDERNEATH OUT OF BOUNDS

Ron Jirsa, Assistant Mens Coach,
Clemson University,
Clemson, S.C.

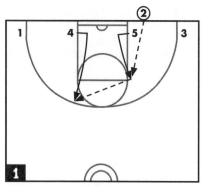

DIAGRAM 1: Initial Movement (Option A). All four players align along the baseline with 3 and 1 in a corner behind the 3-point line, 4 and 5 on opposite low blocks and 2 inbounding the ball. When 2 calls "break," 4 and 5 both cut to the basket and then break up to each elbow. 2 inbounds to 5, who quickly reverses the ball to 4.

DIAGRAM 3: Initial Movement (Option C). As another option, 5 slides across the lane and sets a screen for 4 who pops across the lane to the ball-side elbow. After setting the screen, 5 slides up to the weak-side elbow. 2 throws an inbound pass to 4. 4 quickly swings the ball to 5.

DIAGRAM 2: Initial Movement (Option B). From the same set, 4 and 5 could also criss-cross from the low block to the opposite elbows. 2 passes to 4 at the ball-side elbow. 4 quickly swings the ball to 5.

DIAGRAM 4: First Scoring Option. 2 steps inbound and sets a screen for 3, who runs a flex cut toward the basket. 5 looks to hit 3 for a quick layup.

DIAGRAM 5: Second Scoring Option. After setting the screen for 3, 2 comes off a downscreen from 4

and pops to the top. 5 hits 2 for a jump shot.

DIAGRAM 6:Alternate Entry. 4 and 5 use any of the three initial movement options to get to the elbows. 2 passes to 3, while 4 and 5 break to the basket and set staggered screens for 2, who comes

off the screens and pops to the top of the key. 3 passes to 2 for an open jumper

This is a great under-the-basket inbounds set that offers three ways to get good looks against a tough man-to-man defense.

"TWO" FROM BOX SET

Mike Mullins, Basketball Coach,
Stowers Breakers,
Gadsen, Ala.

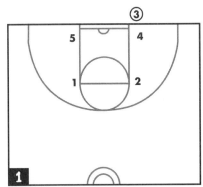

DIAGRAM 1: Players set up in a box alignment with 4 and 5 at the low block on each side of the lane, while 1 and 2 line up at each elbow.

DIAGRAM 2: 5 and 1 cut to the ball side and 4 cuts to the ball-side corner behind the 3-point line. 1 screens for 2 who comes around the top of the screen and cuts toward the baseline on

the weak side.

The first option is for 3 to throw a bounce pass to 2 cutting into the lane if an opening occurs. If that isn't open, then 3 should also look for 2 in the short corner for a quick jump shot. The inbounder can also look for 5 or 4 on the strong side and look to 1 as a safety release if no one is open.

"DUKE" UNDER-THE-BASKET INBOUNDS

Amanda Brown, Head Girls Coach,
Chapin High School,
New York, N.Y.

DIAGRAM 1: This play provides two 3-point options, safe passes and a quick hitter off a screen. If no shot is taken, it's easy to reset into any offense. 2 is on the ball-side low block, 1 is at the ball-side elbow, 5 is on the weak-side elbow and 3 is stationed on the weak side. 3 should be a good 3-point shooter.

DIAGRAM 2: 2 sets an upscreen for 5 who uses the screen and breaks across the lane toward the ball. 1 cuts to the top of the key and 3 breaks behind the 3-point circle on the weak side.

DIAGRAM 3: 4 inbounds to 3 for a quick 3-point shot (3 is the first option), hits 1 for a 3-pointer (second option) or a quick throw in to 5 for a power-up move on the block. 1 can also act as a safety release for the inbounds pass.

After making the pass, 4 cuts inbounds behind 5 on the weak-side short corner to create balance.

> *"The will to win is grossly overrated. The will to prepare is far more important."*
>
> —*Bobby Knight*

"FLASH HARD" UNDERNEATH OUT OF BOUNDS

Greg Siesel, Varsity Coach,
Monroeville High School,
Monroeville, Ohio

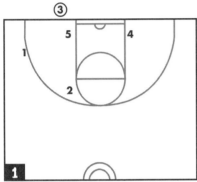

DIAGRAM 1: In the initial setup with 3 inbounding the ball, 4 and 5 line up on opposite low-post blocks. 1 lines up in the ball-side corner and 2 lines up just above the ball-side elbow.

DIAGRAM 3: 4 and 1 set a double screen across the lane for 5 who pops up near the top of the key on the ball side. 2 passes to 5. 3 ducks in behind 4's screen along the side of the lane on the ball side. 5 passes to 3.

DIAGRAM 2: 5 sets a cross screen for 4 who breaks toward the ball and posts up on the ball-side block. 1 sets a screen for 2 who breaks into the ball-side corner behind the 3-point circle. 3 passes to 2.

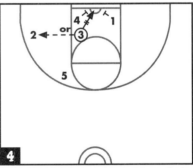

DIAGRAM 4: 4 and 1 curl from their screens and roll toward the basket. 3 can take the shot or kick it back out to 2 for an open jump shot. On any shot, 4 and 1 box out for the rebound.

"BOXER" UNDER-THE-BASKET INBOUNDS

Jerry Coulter,
Powder River County High School,
Broadus, Mont.

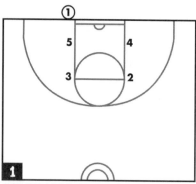

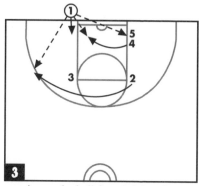

DIAGRAM 1: From a box-set formation, 1 the inbounder, slaps the ball to initiate the action.

coming to the ball for a left-hand layup. 1 may also pass to 2 for the jump shot as the third option.

DIAGRAM 2: 5 and 3 screen across at the same time, 5 screens 4's defender and 3 screens 2's defender.

DIAGRAM 3: 1 looks to pass the ball to 5, who reverse pivots under the basket for a right-hand layup.

The next option is to look for 4

DIAGRAM 4: 1 passes to safety outlet 3, who quickly passes back to 1 after looking faking a pass to 2 in the corner.

1 steps into the middle of the key and sometimes gets an easy basket or draws a foul.

LINE OUT OF BOUNDS

DuWayne Krause
Immanuel Lutheran School
Marshfield, Wis.

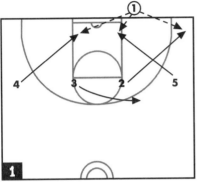

or she can shoot or pass to 5 posting up. 3 acts as a safety release on top.

DIAGRAM 1: Run this play to take advantage of defenders who play too high and tight to their players. 4 and 5 often get easy layups on this play. 2 must be a good shooter who cuts right behind 5. If 2 gets the inbounds pass, he

DIAGRAM 2: The alignment is reversible. It can be run either way without moving the position of players.

PLAY AMERICA

Gene Keady, Head Mens Coach,
Purdue University,
Lafayette, Ind.

DIAGRAM 1: On the slap of the ball, 2 pops across the lane. 2 and 5 set staggered screens for 4. 4 uses both screen and breaks hard to the basket.

After 4's break, 2 curls around 5 and breaks toward the ball. 1 looks to pass to 4 or 2. If neither player is open, 1 hits 3 as a safety release over the top.

M-SERIES, Z-SERIES LOW-HIGH OUT-OF-BOUNDS PLAYS

Kenneth Adams, Retired Coach,
Temple, Ga.

This is a formation that can be used against either a man-to-man or zone defense. The man plays are called M-low or M-high, while the zone plays are called Z-low and Z-high. The numbers in the diagrams can be any player and aren't position specific.

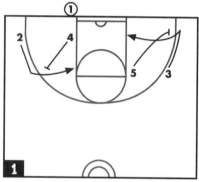

DIAGRAM 1: M-Low. This play begins with 2 and 4 moving up simultaneously, while 3 and 5 are moving down to the weak side. 4 angles toward 2 at the free-throw line extended. 5 angles toward 3 at the block extended.

4 screens for 2 who breaks toward the basket at the high post on the strong side. 5 screens for 3 who uses the screen and breaks toward the basket from the weak side. Players must come off the screens at the same time

DIAGRAM 2: M-High. 3 and 5 start low on the weak side and both break up at the same time. 2 and 4 align side by side in the strong-side wing area at the elbow extended. 2 cuts off 4, looks for a quick pass from 1, goes through the lane and sets a screen for 3 on the

low block.

3 comes off the staggered screens set by 5 and 2 and breaks to the basket. 4 sets a back screen for 5 who rolls off the screen and breaks through the lane and to the ball on the strong-side low block.

DIAGRAM 3: Z-Low. 2 V-cuts up and then into the short corner. 4 screens the defense on the baseline, then slides across the lane for rebounding position. 1 passes to 2 in the short corner, while 5 breaks across the high post to an open area on the ball side. 3 slides to the top of the key and stays back for possible defensive transition.

1 passes to 2 and steps in looking for a return pass and quick shot. 2 has the option to shoot or look for 1 or 5 for a quick shot.

DIAGRAM 4: Z-High. 2 runs a loop under 4 as 4 breaks to the ball-side corner. 2 cuts to the top. 3 and 5 set a double screen on the weak-side low block just as 1 inbounds to 4.

After making the pass, 1 breaks to the weak-side corner cutting off the double screen by 3 and 4. 4 passes to 2, who swings it to 1 for an open jumper.

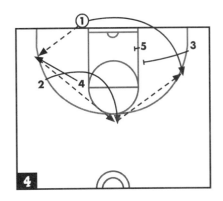

BASELINE OUT-OF-BOUNDS PLAY

Steve Smith, Head Boys Coach,
Oak Hill Academy,
Mouth Of Wilson, Va.

DIAGRAM 1: 2 takes the ball out underneath. 4 sets a cross screen for 5, who breaks under the basket to the weak side. 3 sets a cross screen for 1 who uses the screen and releases behind the 3-point line on the ball side. After setting the screen, 3 rolls a few steps toward the basket.

DIAGRAM 2: 2 looks for 4, 3 or 5 for a high-percentage shot in the lane.

If no one is open, 2 throws to 1 as a safety release.

3-LOW STACK

Nate Webber, Head Boys Coach,
Nottingham High School, Trenton, N.J.

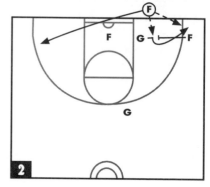

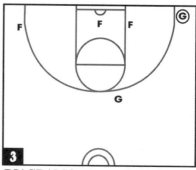

DIAGRAM 1: This out-of-bounds attack is run with three forwards and two guards. Your point guard is at the top. The guard in the lane screens for the forward on the block who rolls to the basket looking for a quick catch-and-shoot opportunity.

DIAGRAM 2: The forward in the corner sets a cross screen for the guard on the block, who uses the screen and pops to the ball-side corner. The forward inbounds to either the ball-side guard or forward and then breaks to the weak-side corner.

DIAGRAM 3: The guard with the ball can now take an open 3-point shot or kick the ball back to the top for a possible ball reversal into the opposite corner. The forward under the basket should box out and try to secure any rebounds.

"Ask not what your teammates can do for you. Ask what you can do for your teammates."

—*Magic Johnson*

"4-DIVE" UNDERNEATH OUT-OF-BOUNDS

Nate Webber, Head Boys Coach,
Nottingham High School, Trenton, N.J.

DIAGRAM 1: 3 inbounds the ball, while 2 and 5 line up on the low-post blocks. 4 sets up at the middle of the foul line and 1 sets up at the ball-side elbow. On the slap of the ball, 2 breaks to the ball-side corner behind the 3-point line, 1 pops out to the top beyond the 3-point circle and 5 breaks up to set a screen for 4.

DIAGRAM 2: 4 uses 5's screen, reads the defense to see what the best cutting angle is and breaks down the lane toward the basket looking for the quick inbound pass from 3 for a layup.

DIAGRAM 3: Option. From the same set, 5 breaks up and sets a screen for 4. 3 throws an inbound pass in to 2 in the corner. While the pass is being made, 4 uses 5's screen and breaks to the basket and sets a screen for 3 coming inbounds. 2 passes to 1 who swings the ball to 3 coming off 4's screen for an open 3-point shot.

"When you face a fork in the road, step on the accelerator!"

—*Pat Riley*

1-4 LOW ATTACK WITH MULTIPLE OPTIONS

Nathan Livesay, Head Coach,
A.C. Flora High School,
Columbia, S.C.

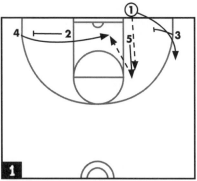

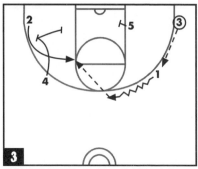

DIAGRAM 1: Option 1. From a 1-4 low set with 1 inbounding the ball under the basket, 1 first looks for a quick lob pass to 5 for a layup. If this option isn't there, 5 pops to the elbow and receives the pass from 1.

On 5's catch, 3 screens down for 1 and 2 sets a flex screen for 4.

DIAGRAM 3: Option 2 (Continued). If 5 isn't open, 3 swings the ball to 1. 4 sets a downscreen for 2. 1 takes a few hard dribbles out to the top and looks for 2 coming open off the screen.

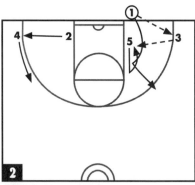

DIAGRAM 2: Option 2. If 1 is unable to inbound to 5, 1 passes to 3 in the corner. 1 steps in and sets an upscreen for 5. 2 and 4 interchange to occupy the weak-side defense. 3 looks to hit 5 in the post.

DIAGRAM 4: Option 3. 1 makes an inbound pass to 4 on the weak-side corner. After the inbound pass, 1 comes hard off a triple screen set by 5, 3 and 2 and breaks to the top.

DIAGRAM 5: Option 3 (Continued). 4 passes to 1. 1 can either shoot an open jumper, make a return pass to 4 cutting backdoor or look to pass to 2 off the double-flare screen set by 3 and 5 on the opposite wing.

MULTI-SCREEN OUT-OF-BOUNDS PLAY

Mike Pendleton, Assistant Coach,
Fresno Pacific University,
Fresno, Calif.

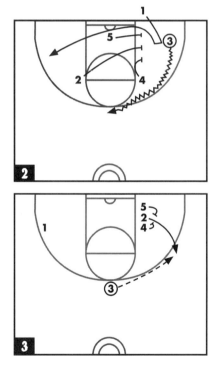

DIAGRAM 1: Initial formation is out of a box set. 5 screens across for 3 to receive the entry pass from 1.

DIAGRAM 2: Player 3 starts dribbling out high, looking for 1 to come off a triple screen set by 5, 2 and 4. If open, 3 passes to 1. But this is usually just a decoy to set up the actual play.

DIAGRAM 3: Players 5 and 4 screen in for 2 who splits the screens and receives a pass from 3 for an open 3-point shot.

If 2 can't get a shot off, 4 or 5 can fade to the back-side block where a basic 3-2 motion (2 post motion) offense begins.

"XAVIER" VS. MAN-TO-MAN

Kirk Kaul, Head Boys Coach,
Hustisford High School,
Hustisford, Wis.

This under-the-basket inbounds play has worked almost every time for our team.

DIAGRAM 1: The player on the ball-side block pops to the corner and acts as a decoy. He or she then rolls deep and serves as a defensive safety. The player at the weak-side elbow dives to the ball looking for the inbounds pass. If there's no pass, then that player goes to the ball-side corner.

The player on the weak-side low block pops up and sets an upscreen for the player on the ball-side elbow. The player on the ball-side elbow curls

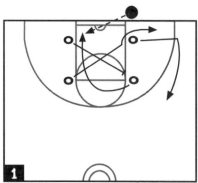

around the screen and breaks to the opposite block to catch the inbound pass and score.

INBOUND "X" SERIES

Billy Schmidt, Former Coach,
Northwestern University,
Evanston, Ill.

DIAGRAM 1: This is the basic set. 5 is a wildcard and can be used as a screener or as the primary option.

DIAGRAM 2: 3 takes the ball out of bounds. 2 sets a diagonal screen for 4 cutting to the post. 5 sets a cross screen

for 2. The pass to 2 is our first option. 1 V-cuts to the top.

DIAGRAM 3: 3 steps inbounds and looks to seal the defender inside. If 3 is not open immediately, 2 passes to 1. On the pass to 1, 5 comes off a baseline

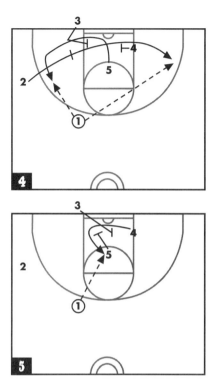

screen from 4 to receive the pass from 1. 5 can shoot or look for 4 on the block.

DIAGRAM 4: We'll run this action as a counter. On the pass from 2 to 1, 5 drops to the baseline then curls off a double screen from 3 and 2. 2 then clears to the opposite wing off a screen from 4. 1 can pass to either 5 or 2.

DIAGRAM 5: Another counter to the original action is to have 3 and 5 set a double screen for 4. 4 curls around the double screen and receives a pass from 1 for a shot from inside the lane.

BASELINE SERIES: 5 PLAYS FROM THE SAME SET

Marty Gaughan, Head Boys Coach,
Benet Academy,
Lisle, Ill.

We run five inbound plays from the same set. Each play is run for a specific player on the floor. For example, play No. 1 is run for player 1, etc. This gives us flexibility to run a play to any player and makes us difficult to scout because these plays are all run from the same inbounds set.

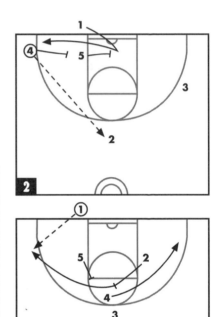

DIAGRAM 1: Play No. 1. 5 screens for 4 and then rolls back toward the basket. 4 breaks to the ball-side corner. 3 sets a downscreen for 2 and cuts to the weak side. 2 cuts to the top.

DIAGRAM 2: Play No. 1 (Continued). 4 throws a quick swing pass to 2. 1 steps inbounds and acts as if he or she is going to the weak-side corner, but then cuts back to the ball-side corner. 2 fakes a pass to 3, then throws the ball to 1 in the corner for a quick shot.

DIAGRAM 3: Play No. 2. 2 breaks and sets an upscreen for 4 who cuts to the weak-side corner. 5 screens-the-screener for 2 who uses 5's screen and cuts to the ball-side behind the 3-point line. 3 sets a downscreen for 2, then breaks to the top and serves as a safety release. 1 passes to 2 for a quick 3-point shot.

DIAGRAM 4: Play No. 3. 4 breaks into the weak-side corner, while 3 cuts down the lane and sets a downscreen for 2 who comes off the screen and pops to the top of the key. 5 cuts to the ball-side corner and receives an inbound pass from 1. 5 immediately swings the ball to 2 out top.

DIAGRAM 5: Play No. 3 (Continued). 1 comes inbound and cuts to the

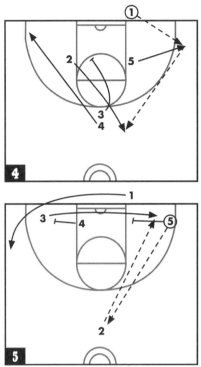

4

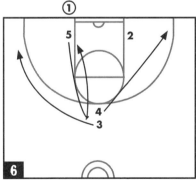

5

weak-side corner and yells for the ball. 4 and 5 set staggered screens along the baseline for 3 who cuts to the short corner on the ball side. 2 fakes a pass to 1 and throws it to 3 coming off the staggered screens. 3 catches and shoots a short, baseline jump shot.

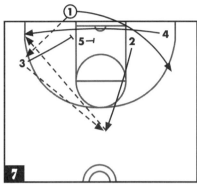

6

DIAGRAM 6: Play No. 4. 5 pops to the top and sets a screen for 3 who cuts

to the ball-side corner. After setting the screen, 5 rolls back toward the inbounder calling for the ball. 4 breaks to the weak-side corner.

7

DIAGRAM 7: Play No. 4 (Continued). 1 inbounds to 3 who immediately swings the ball to 2 popping out to the top. 4 cuts across the lane and breaks into the corner off staggered screens set by 5 and 3. 2 passes to 4 who shoots a baseline jump shot.

8

DIAGRAM 8: Play No. 5. 3 releases up top and acts as a safety release. 5 pops up and sets a screen for 4 who breaks into the ball-side corner. As 5 is setting the screen, 2 slides across the lane and sets an upscreen for 5 (screen-the-screener action). 5 curls around 2's screen and breaks to the basket looking for the inbound pass from 1 for a catch-and-shoot opportunity.

ENDLINE OB PLAY

Vinod Vachani,
Welham Girls' High School,
Dehra Dun, India

DIAGRAM 1: 5, 4 and 2 break from a triple stack formation. 3 fakes one way and cuts the opposite way around the stack and into the lane. 5 releases around 4 and 2 and heads toward the ball. 4 moves last, out to the perimeter. 1 passes to 3, 5 or 4.

DIAGRAM 2: If the initial options fail, 1 inbounds to 4. 2 flashes out to the perimeter to receive a pass from 4. 4 downscreens for 1 stepping inbounds. 2 passes to 1 for the open shot.

"THE LINE" INBOUNDS SERIES

Mike Feagans,
Rensselaer Central High School,
Rensselaer, Ind.

This endline out-of-bounds series allows teams a quick hitter for a 3-pointer or layup, depending on what you need at the time. The set is designed with 4 players lining up on the free-throw line. Design the positions to fit your team.

DIAGRAM 1: Option A. When 3 slaps the ball, 4 and 5 come together to set a double screen for 1, who cuts to the opposite block looking for a quick layup. 2 steps back as a safety valve.

DIAGRAM 2: Option B. When 3 slaps the ball, 4 cuts to the ball-side block and 5 cuts to the opposite block. 4 and 5 cross paths to confuse the defense. 2 steps back for the release pass, 1 cuts to the corner.

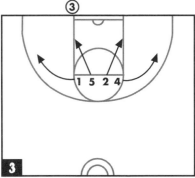

DIAGRAM 3: Option C. 1, 5, 2 and 4 cut to their designated spots as soon as the ball is given to 3.

DIAGRAM 4: Option D. 2 sets a screen for 4 cutting to the ball and runs off a double screen from 5 and 1.

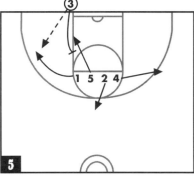

DIAGRAM 5: Option E. 1 steps out along the free-throw line extended to receive the entry pass. 3 steps in to set a screen for 5 cutting to the block. 2 steps out to the top, 4 steps out to the opposite wing.

"Everyone is born with a certain potential. You may never achieve your full potential, but how close you come depends on how much you want to pay the price."

—*Red Auerbach*

"2-DELAY" UNDER-THE-BASKET PLAY

Ron Newquist,
Illinois Wolverines AAU,
Chicago Heights, Ill.

DIAGRAM 1: Your best shooter should inbound the ball (2 in this case). 4 downscreens for 3. 3 comes off the screen and pops out behind the 3-point line. 1 sets at the free-throw line and 5 acts as a safety release behind the 3-point line in the backcourt.

DIAGRAM 2: 2 inbounds to 3. 4 posts up on the ball-side block. 1 makes a V-cut and pops out to the top of the key. 5 continues to float behind the 3-point line in the backcourt. 4 may have a good look on the post up and 3 should look to 4 as the first option.

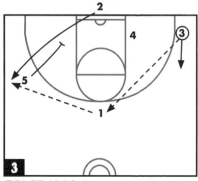

DIAGRAM 3: 3 passes to 1. 5 sets a downscreen for player 2. As soon as 1 catches the pass, 2 comes off 5's screen and receives a pass from 1.

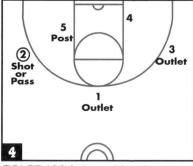

DIAGRAM 4: 2 can either shoot or pass to 5, who is posting up on the block. 3 and 1 serve as outlets if neither 2 or 5 is open.

Timing is the key for this play, as 2 must come off the screen just as the pass arrives.

MULTI-OPTION, OUT-OF-BOUNDS PLAY

Bill Kunze,
Duluth East High School,
Duluth, Minn.

DIAGRAM 1: Initial set.

DIAGRAM 2: 3 cuts to the ball-side block. 5 breaks up to the foul line and sets a screen for 1 who breaks ball side behind the 3-point line at the foul-line extended. 2 passes in to 1.

DIAGRAM 3: After the entry pass, 2 cuts inbound directly under the basket. 5 cuts to the ball-side block area. 4 sets a screen for 2 on the weak side, while 3 and 5 set staggered screens for 2 on the ball side. Depending on the defense, 2 can use either screen and try to come free. 1 dribbles right and looks to hit 2 with a pass coming off any of the screens.

DIAGRAM 4: Counter Play. From the same look, 2 passes to 1 and cuts straight up to the top. 5 curls around 3 and breaks to the ball-side corner. 4 breaks across the lane and sets a screen for 3, who can either curl around the screen and look for an opening in the middle of the lane or break to the weak-side short corner. After setting the screen for 3, 4 breaks to the ball-side block and posts up.

1 passes to 2. 2 has multiple options including throwing a pass to 5 in the corner, hitting 4 in the post or passing to 3 coming either way off 4's screen.

1-2-2 DISGUISE SERIES

Ron Brown, Retired Head Coach,
Machias Memorial High School,
Machias, Maine

Here's an underneath-the-basket series that's been really successful for our team. There are three plays in the series and they work because they look and start the same, but end differently. This makes them tough for our opponents to scout.

and receive the inbound pass for a quick shot.

This option is especially effective at the end of a game, quarter or half.

DIAGRAM 1: Play A. Once the official hands the ball to 1, 1 slaps it and initiates the action. 2 cuts up the lane diagonally to set a screen for 5. 5 cuts to the basket looking for the inbound pass and a quick layup. 4 pops out to the top and acts as a safety release for 1 to throw to.

DIAGRAM 2: Play B. The beauty of this series is the attention that 5 receives by the defense. Once your opponent has seen this play, they'll focus their attention on stopping 5. Have 2 move beyond the 3-point arc

DIAGRAM 3: Play B (Continued). The defenders will be focused on 5 and 3 down low. 1 throws the pass over the top of the defense, hitting 2 for an open catch-and-shoot for 3-points.

"ALPHA-BETA-DELTA" OUT OF BOX SET

Peter Harris,
Kansas City College & Bible School
Overland Park, Kan.

DIAGRAM 1: "Alpha." 1 and 2 line up on the blocks and post players at the elbows. Both guards screen for the forwards who crash the lane looking for the ball. 1 cross screens for 2 who breaks out to the perimeter.

DIAGRAM 2: "Beta." 1 receives the pass from 3. 4 and 5 set a double screen for 2, who pops to the free-throw line to receive a pass from 1. 2 either passes to the cutting post players or skip passes to 3 coming to the corner.

DIAGRAM 3: "Delta." 3 inbounds to 4 then clears into the corner. 1 sets a cross screen for 2. 4 looks to either 2 coming around 1's screen or to 5 cutting hard down the lane.

"Keep it simple. When you get too complicated, you forget the obvious."

—*Al McGuire*

"BRUIN" WITH COUNTERS

Jimmy Brown, Former Head Coach,
Georgia Southern,
Statesboro, Ga.

DIAGRAM 1: As soon as the ball is handed to 1 by the official, your players must begin their breaks. 3 cuts ahead of 2 and breaks for the basket. 4 and 5 set a double screen for 2, who comes off the screens and receives the inbound pass for an open jumper from the wing. 1 looks for 3 first, then 2.

DIAGRAM 3: Counter 1. Line up the same way as before. When the ball is handed to 1, 3 fakes going over the top of the double screens and breaks back to the ball-side wing. 2 fakes going around the top of the screens and V-cuts back toward the basket. The second option remains the same.

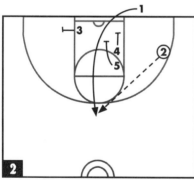

DIAGRAM 2: If 2 gets the ball, but doesn't have a clear shot, 4 and 5 roll toward the basket and set a double screen for 1 breaking inbounds and popping to the top of the key. 2 quickly swings the ball to 1 for the open shot at the top of the key.

DIAGRAM 4: Counter 2. From the same alignment, 4 breaks to the opposite block and 5 fills 4's spot. 1 looks for either 4 or 5 down low. If the defense is used to 4 and 5 being screeners from this alignment, it may catch them off guard.

FLEXIBLE INBOUNDS PLAY

Weldon Bradshaw,
Collegiate School,
Richmond, Va.

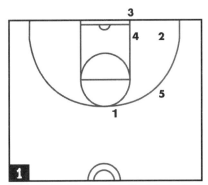

DIAGRAM 1: 3 makes the inbounds pass. 4 lines up in the second lane space facing 3. 2 lines up about five-feet away from 4 facing the baseline. 1 and 5 line up on the perimeter near the 3-point arc.

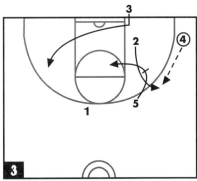

DIAGRAM 3: After setting the screen, 2 uses a screen from 5 to get a swing pass from 4. 3 steps in and looks for a quick post-up opportunity, then clears to the weak side. 5 should look for a seam and post up after screening for 2.

DIAGRAM 2: 3 slaps the ball to start the play. 4 attempts to gain position for a direct pass from 3, but if nothing opens up, 4 pops out to the corner off a screen from 2. 1 should flash into the lane to draw the defense and then pop back out as a safety valve.

DIAGRAM 4: If 2 doesn't have an open shot, swing the ball 2 to 1 to 3 for a shot on the other wing. If 3 isn't open, flow into a basic offensive set.

POINT CURL

Marty Cline,
North Hopkins High School,
Madisonville, Ky.

We've averaged three good shots a game off this play. Most defenses think 1 will just pop out as the safety — that's what makes this play successful.

DIAGRAM 2: 5 turns and sets a screen for 1. 1 curls outside of the lane for a 10-foot jumper. 5 drops out as safety. 3 posts for rebound.

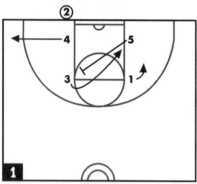

DIAGRAM 1: 4 pops to the corner. 5 sets a diagonal upscreen for 3 who goes to the opposite block.

OUT-OF-BOUNDS SERIES

Paul C. Hill,
Tennessee Temple University,
Chattanooga, Tenn.

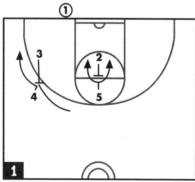

DIAGRAM 1: 2 upscreens for 5, who reads the defense and goes to either side. 3 screens for 4, then slides to an open area.

DIAGRAM 2: 2 screens for 5 just like in Diagram 1, but then 3 and 4 set a double screen for 2 for a 3-point shot or curl to the basket.

DIAGRAM 3: 2 upscreens for 5, who goes to the basket. 2 then slides to set another screen for 4. 3 screens for 2 for a 3-point shot.

DIAGRAM 4: 3 upscreens for 4. 2 and 5 come together and double screen for 3 who curls to the basket for a layup.

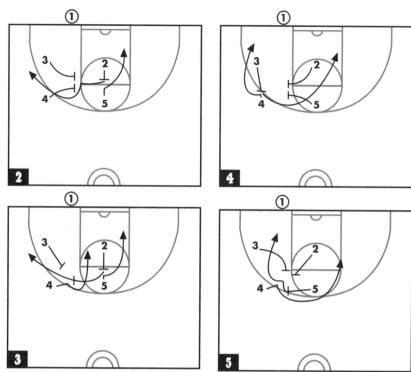

DIAGRAM 5: 5 comes across and sets a pick for 4. 3 and 2 set a double screen for 5, who rolls to the basket for a layup.

"NINE" BOX-SET INBOUND

Bill Kunze,
Duluth East High School,
Duluth, Minn.

The first year we ran this play we scored 9 straight baskets, so we call it "nine."
DIAGRAM 1: 5 fakes into the lane, then cuts to the corner for the pass from 1. 2 drops down next to 4 to help set a double screen for 1. 5 receives the pass and shoots a shot or passes over to 1 for the shot. 3 V-cuts to become the safety release player.

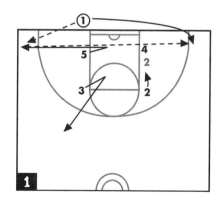

"GEORGIA" OUT-OF-BOUNDS PLAY (VS. ZONE)

Andy Landers, Head Womens Coach,
University of Georgia,
Athens, Ga.

DIAGRAM 1: Player 1 inbounds and 5 lines up behind the 3-point line on the ball side. You'll also position a wing player (W) on the ball-side block, a shooter (S) at the ball-side elbow and post player (P) on the weak-side block.

DIAGRAM 3: 1 passes to W. 5 pops up to the ball-side elbow and S breaks toward W.

DIAGRAM 2: 5 sets a screen for W who comes off the screen and curls all the way into the baseline corner.

DIAGRAM 4: 1 steps inbounds and sets a screen for W. W can use 1's screen and shoot a 3-pointer from the corner or pass to S for a quick open jumper.

UNDER-THE-BASKET INBOUNDS VS. ZONE

Donnie Hand,
Chilton High School,
Clanton, Ala.

DIAGRAM 1: This is a great play to use, especially against a 1-2-2 zone. 4 and 1 line up under the basket. 3 and 5 line up at the elbows. 1 loops around to the top of the key. 4 breaks toward the ball and posts up on the block. If 4 can't get good position, then 4 slides into the corner. (Hopefully, the defender will follow.)

DIAGRAM 2: While 4 is sliding to the corner, 3 breaks down the lane filling 4's position on the block. If the low-post defender follows 4, then 3 should be open. 5 breaks to the backside block. 5 should be open if the backside defender helps with 3.

DIAGRAM 3: 2 can pass to 3 or 5 on the blocks, 4 in the corner or 1 as an outlet if no one is open.

"Conceive the inconceivable
— then accomplish it."

—*Jim Valvano*

"WHITE" INBOUNDS UNDER THE BASKET
(VS. MAN OR ZONE)

Mike Mullins, Head Coach,
Stowers Breakers Girls Team,
Gadsden, Ala.

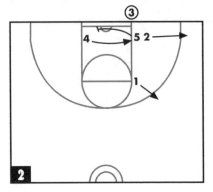

DIAGRAM 1: This is the initial setup. 5 and 2 line up directly in front of 3. 4 sets up on the opposite block and 1 lines up at the elbow.

3 should be an athletic player who's very aggressive going to the basket.

DIAGRAM 2: 5 breaks across the lane and sets a screen for 4, who breaks off the screen and rolls toward the inbounder. 2 cuts to the ball-side corner. 1 releases to the wing area as a safety release on the inbound pass.

DIAGRAM 3: 3 looks to pass to 4 breaking toward the ball or 5 on the opposite block. If neither player is open, 3 passes to 2 or 1. If 1 or 2 receives the pass, then 3 steps in and looks for a quick lob pass from either player.

UNDERNEATH OUT-OF-BOUNDS PLAY (VS. MAN OR ZONE)

Pat Sullivan, Head Mens Coach,
St. Francis University,
Joliet, Ill.

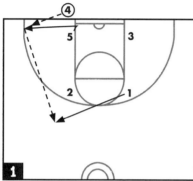

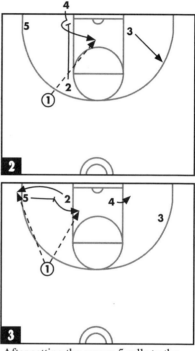

DIAGRAM 1: 4 inbounds the ball, while 2 and 1 are at the elbows and 5 and 3 are on the blocks. 5 steps in, then busts to the corner. 1 pops out to the top on the ball side. 4 passes to 5, 5 passes to 1.

DIAGRAM 2: 2 sets a downscreen for 4 who is coming inbounds. If the defense is man-to-man, 2 screens 4's defender. If they're in a zone defense, 2 screens the middle defender in the zone. 4 curls off 2's screen and looks for a pass from 1.

DIAGRAM 3: 5 screens-the-screener and 2 pops to the ball-side corner.

After setting the screen 5 rolls to the basket. 1 looks for 2 or throws a "jump-shot pass" to 5 in the post.

"Play the game with a smile."

—*Earl "The Pearl" Monroe*

UNDER-THE-BASKET INBOUNDS PLAY (VS. MAN OR ZONE)

Melody Owsley,
Racine Prairie High School,
Racine, Wis

This play works well against either
man or zone defenses.

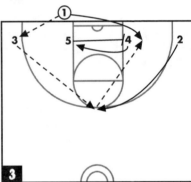

DIAGRAM 1: Against man-to-man, 5
screens for 4 then reverse pivots for a
right-handed layup or possible foul.

DIAGRAM 2: Against a zone, 5
screens away for 4 and reverse pivots.
If 5 is not open, 5 should pin the low
post defender for the pass to 2 for a
shot in the corner.

DIAGRAM 3: A second option
against both man or zone defenses. 5
screens across and pins the defender as
4 comes to the ball. 1 inbounds to 3 as
2 slides to the top of the key. 1 enters
the play and comes off the screen by 5
for the shot.

---

*"Any team can be a miracle team, but you
have to go out and work for your miracles."*

—Pat Riley

SCOREBOARD SCORCHERS

BASELINE OUT-OF-BOUNDS PLAY (VS. MAN)

Andy Landers, Head Womens Coach,
University of Georgia,
Athens, Ga.

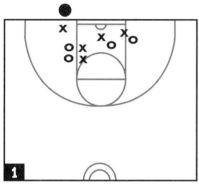

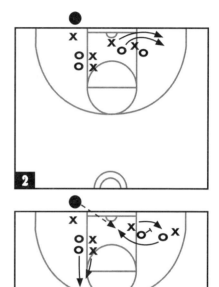

DIAGRAM 1: Stack two players on the foul line at the mid-post area. Align a player in the lane on the low post and have another player on the weak-side low block.

DIAGRAM 2: When the inbounder calls "Break!" the player in the lane slashes to the weak-side short corner. In a man-to-man defense, his or her defender will follow.

DIAGRAM 3: The player on the weak-side low block immediately steps up and sets a back screen on the slashing player's defender. The slashing player stops and quickly rolls over the top of the screen and back to the basket. The defense rarely has enough time to execute a proper switch and will both get caught up in the screen. The rolling player will be open for a easy catch-and-score. Defensive help from anywhere else leaves another player wide open.

> *"You're not going to win with the kids who are just All-Americans. The kids must have more than status, they must have togetherness."*
>
> —*John Thompson*

BOX-SET OUT OF BOUNDS (VS. MAN)

Allen Osborne,
Poca High School,
Poca, W.Va.

Run this play to get quick opportunities for your best post player (5) and best shooter (2).

DIAGRAM 1: 5 inbounds the ball to 1 coming off a screen from 2. 5 steps in on the block and posts-up looking for a

pass from 1. 3 and 4 set a double screen at the foul line.

DIAGRAM 2: 1 looks inside to 5 posting. If this is not available, 1 dribbles away from the baseline looking for 2 coming off the double screen.

UNDERNEATH OUT-OF-BOUNDS PLAY (VS. ZONE)

Tega Carter,
Oak Ridge Military Academy,
Oak Ridge, N. C.

DIAGRAM 1: 3 inbounds the ball, while 1, 2, 4 and 5 form a stack along the ball-side lane line.

DIAGRAM 2: 1 fakes left, then V-cuts to the right and breaks all the way to the top of the key. 2 fakes an inside break to the basket and flares to the ball-side corner behind the 3-point line.

DIAGRAM 3: 4 clears out X5 (this isn't a screen, he or she just gets low and clears X5 out of the way). 5 steps up and looks for a quick inbounds pass for a layup. In this set, against this defense,

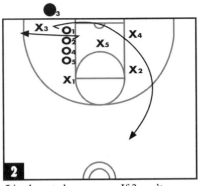

5 is almost always open. If 3 can't inbound to 5, he or she looks to 2 for an open 3-pointer or passes to 1 at the top of the key.

UNDER-THE-BASKET INBOUNDS (VS. MAN)

Brent Brannon, Assistant Boys Coach,
Calhoun High School,
Calhoun, Ga.

DIAGRAM 1: 2 fakes into the middle and curls around stack off 4 and 5 looking for the ball. As 2 clears, 4 and 5 set staggered screens for 1. 3 passes to 1.

DIAGRAM 2: As 1 catches the ball, 4 and 5 set a staggered screen for 2 who comes to the point. 1 passes to 2.

DIAGRAM 3: As 2 catches the pass, 4 and 5 then set baseline stagger screens for 3 who sets the defense up with a V-cut. 2 hits 3 for the shot.

"40" BOX SET OUT-OF-BOUNDS PLAY (VS. MAN)

Rusty Evans,
Heard County High School,
Franklin, Ga.

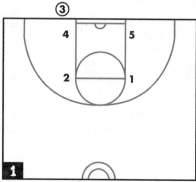

DIAGRAM 1: Initial set. 3 takes the ball out. 4 and 5 line up on the blocks just outside the lane. 1 and 2 set up on the elbows.

DIAGRAM 2: 4 rolls and sets a high screen for 2, who pops to the corner. 1 pops to the top of the key. 5 remains on the low weak-side block.

DIAGRAM 3: 5 cuts across the lane and sets a back screen on 4's defender, then rolls toward the ball. 4 comes off the back screen and cuts to the weak-side block. 3 tries to hit 4 for an easy layup. 2 remains in the corner and 1 tries to remain near the top of the key area.

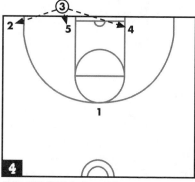

DIAGRAM 4: 3 now has 2, 5 or 4 for scoring options along the baseline. 1 remains as a pressure release near the top of the key.

Chapter 3

SIDELINE INBOUNDS PLAYS

"TRIANGLE"

Peter Harris, Head Mens Coach,
Kansas City College And Bible School,
Overland Park, Kan.

DIAGRAM 1: 1, 2 and 3 should be your three best perimeter shooters and should be placed in a triangle as shown. 5 inbounds the ball. 4 sets up on the perimeter between 2 and 5.

4 and 2 set staggered screens for 3 (2 must set his or her screen in the middle of the lane) who breaks out to the perimeter to receive the inbounds pass. Immediately after 3 passes by 2's screen, 1 sets a downscreen for 2 who breaks up to the point. After setting the

downscreen, 1 flashes out to the wing.

If 3 isn't open for a shot, he or she passes to 2. If 2 isn't open, he or she swings the ball over to 1.

DIAGRAM 2: If 1 isn't open for a shot, 3 and 4 set staggered screens for 5 who cuts hard to the basket.

Defenses frequently neglect the inbounder, so if all else fails — and if 1, 2 or 3 don't get an open jumper — then 5 should be open for a good shot cutting to the basket.

SIDELINE OUT-OF-BOUNDS: STAGGERED SET SERIES

Bob Baker,
Ashland University,
Ashland, Ohio

The objective of this series is to provide a quick scoring opportunity against an aggressive man-to-man defense.

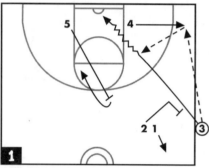

DIAGRAM 1: If 3 is being guarded taking the ball out of bounds, 1 and 2 split. Simultaneously, 4 cuts hard to the corner while 5 cuts to the top of the key. 3 inbounds the ball to 4 and cuts hard to the basket off a back screen from 2. 4 passes to 3. 5 rolls to the opposite block to follow the shot.

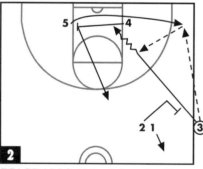

DIAGRAM 2: If the defense is effectively denying the corner entry pass to 4, 4 and 5 can switch roles. If neither entry pass is open, use 1 as a release.

DIAGRAM 3: Another option is to inbound the ball directly to 5. The initial action is the same. After the ball is inbounded to 5, 4 moves up the sideline to back screen for 3 cutting to the basket. 2 back screens for 1. 5 has the option to pass to either 3 or 1 coming off the back screens. 4 rolls to the basket, while 2 serves as a safety release.

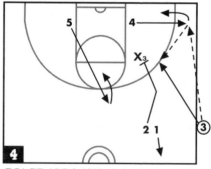

DIAGRAM 4: If 3's defender drops off into the lane, the initial actions remains the same. After the ball is inbounded to 4 in the corner, 2 downscreens for 3. 4 passes to 3 for the open perimeter jumper. 4 and 5 roll to the basket for the rebound. 1 is the safety release.

SIDE-OUT PLAY FOR ANY SITUATION

Tubby Smith, Head Mens Coach,
University of Kentucky,
Lexington, Ky.

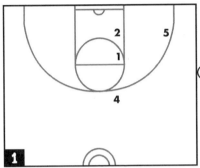

DIAGRAM 1: 3 takes the ball out on the side, while the guards (1 and 2) line up in the lane. 5 lines up on the ball side near the 3-point line and 4 positions him or herself up top beyond the 3-point circle.

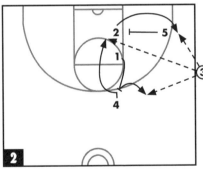

DIAGRAM 2: 1 breaks up and screens for 4, then rolls to the top of the 3-point circle. 4 uses 1's screen and cuts hard to the basket. 5 screens in for

2, who rolls underneath the screen and pops out behind the 3-point line in the ball-side corner. 3 looks for a lob pass to 4 breaking toward the basket or hits 2 in the corner. 2 can either shoot a 3-pointer or dump it in to 5 on the low block for a post-up shot. 1 rolls to the top and acts as a safety outlet for the inbounds passer.

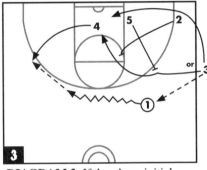

DIAGRAM 3: If there's no initial shot, then 3 inbounds to the safety outlet (1). 1 takes the inbounds pass and dribbles to the left. While 1 is dribbling left, 4 pops out behind the 3-point line at the free-throw line extended. 5 and 2 break up and set staggered screens for 3. 1 passes to 4. 3 can come either over the top or underneath the staggered screens and then cut toward the basket. 4 looks for 3 on either cut to the basket.

SIDELINE SPECIAL

Willie Banks,
Dunbar Vocational High School,
Chicago, Ill.

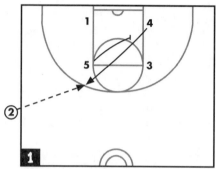

DIAGRAM 1: Players are lined up in a box-set formation with 1 and 4 on opposite low-post blocks and 5 and 3 at the elbows. 2 inbounds the ball and should be your best outside shooter.

2 slaps the ball to start the play and 5 sets a cross screen for 4 who breaks to the ball and receives a pass from 2.

DIAGRAM 2: 1 pops up and sets a back screen for 2. 2 uses the screen and cuts backdoor looking for a quick pass from 4. 3 and 5 remain on the weak side.
DIAGRAM 3: If 2 doesn't receive the pass back from 4, then he or she cuts all the way through the lane and comes

off a double screen set by 3 and 5. 2 must set up his or her defender and get free coming off the double screens.

While 2 is making the cut, 1 breaks to the top of the key and receives a pass back from 4. After setting the screen, 3 breaks to the weak-side.

DIAGRAM 4: 1 passes to 2 for a quick 3-point shot. 2 has several options. He or she can shoot the 3-pointer, throw an entry pass in to 5 for a post-up shot, hit 4 for a free-throw line jumper or throw a skip pass cross court to 3 for a quick jump shot.

"POST" SIDE OUT-OF-BOUNDS PLAY

Wim Cluytens, Head Coach,
Mechelen High School,
Mechelen, Belgium

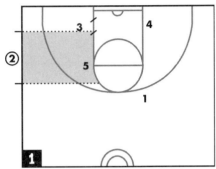

DIAGRAM 1: Have a big guard or forward take the ball out of bounds. 5 posts near the ball-side elbow and 4 sets up on the weak-side low post. This play works best when the inbound point is in the vicinity of the shaded area shown on the diagram.

DIAGRAM 3: If 2 can't get the ball in to 4, he or she should pass to 1. 4 goes to the opposite low post to help set a double pick with 5. 3 fakes the back screen and cuts baseline using the double screen. 1 passes to 3 for the shot.

DIAGRAM 2: 5 turns and screens for 4 coming to the ball-side elbow for the entry pass. As 4 receives the ball, 3 back screens for 2. 2 cuts baseline for a possible layup. 3 may also be open after the screen for an open jumper.

DIAGRAM 4: This is a variation of the play. 5 screens for 4 cutting to the elbow, but now 5 sets a second pick for 3. 3 fakes setting a back screen then turns baseline off the pick from 5. 2 cuts high over 4 and off a screen set by 1 for an open jumper. 4 can pass to 3 near the basket or to 2 for the open shot.

SIDELINE OUT-OF-BOUNDS INTO THE FLEX

Mike Boehme,
Liberty High School,
Eldersburg, Md.

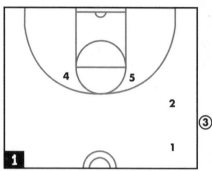

DIAGRAM 1: This is the initial set up with 3 inbounding the ball. 4 and 5 are positioned near both elbows.

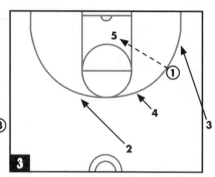

for 1 who drives to the basket. 2 and 4 cut to the elbows.

DIAGRAM 2: 2 back screens for 1 and releases as a safety outlet while 1 cuts to the ball side toward the baseline. 5 screens across for 4 who comes toward the ball while 5 rolls to the basket. 3 inbounds to 1. If 1 is covered, then 3 looks for 2 or 4 for the inbound pass.

DIAGRAM 3: 3 heads toward the corner while 1 looks for 5 rolling to the hoop. 2 and 4 break toward the middle of the floor to even the spacing.

DIAGRAM 4: If 1 can't hit 5 for the layup, then 5 should set a back screen

DIAGRAM 5: If 1 can't get the layup, then he or she should continue to dribble through to the corner. 5 should come to the ball-side block. 1 passes to 2.

DIAGRAM 6: You're now set up to run the flex. 2 passes to 4. 5 steps out and screens for 1 who cuts to the lane. From there, continuous flex-action should take place (2 downscreens for 5 who pops to the elbow, etc.).

"POLAR BEAR" SIDE OUT OF BOUNDS

Greg Siesel, Varsity Coach,
Monroeville High School,
Monroeville, Ohio

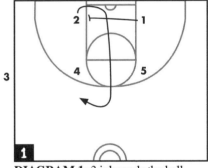

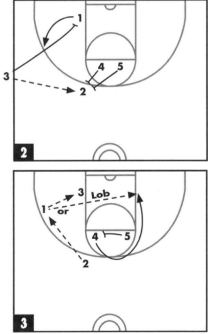

DIAGRAM 1: 3 inbounds the ball from the side. 1 sets a pick for 2. 2 curls around the pick and goes between 4 and 5 to the top of the key.
DIAGRAM 2: 4 and 5 set a double screen for 2. 2 receives entry pass from 3 and looks for immediate shot. After making the pass, 3 downscreens for 1, who comes off the screen and pops into the 3-point area.
DIAGRAM 3: If the initial shot isn't there, 2 passes to 1 who can shoot or pass to 3 for a post up on the low block. 5 sets a pick for 4 who curls around for a possible lob pass from 1.

"FOX" SIDELINE INBOUNDS

Dan Ross, Basketball Coach,
Fox Chapel High School,
Pittsburgh, Pa.

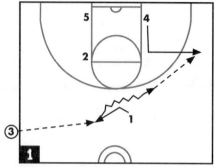

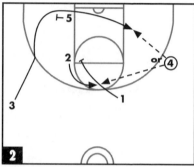

DIAGRAM 1: 3 takes the ball out on the side. 1 makes a hard V-cut to get open and receive the inbound pass. 1 dribbles toward the weak side and passes to 4 sliding up the lane and out to the wing.

DIAGRAM 2: 3 steps inbound and cuts toward the basket off a screen set by 5. 1 sets a downscreen for 2 at the elbow and 2 rolls to the top. 4 passes to either 3 on the low block or 2 at the top of the key.

SIDELINE VS. MAN

Kenneth Adams,
Retired Basketball Coach,
Temple, Ga.

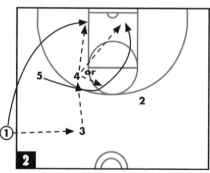

DIAGRAM 1: With 1 inbounding the ball, 2 sets a screen for 3 going hard to the ball. 4 waits for a two count, then sets a screen for 5. Both 4 and 5 break to the wing area at the free-throw line extended.

DIAGRAM 2: Option 1. 1 passes to 3 who hits 4 popping up to the free-throw line extended. 5 cuts off 4 and heads to the basket. 4 either hands the ball off or drops a bounce pass to 5 as he or she makes the break toward the basket.

After making the inbounds pass, 1 makes a backdoor cut to the basket and looks for a pass back from 4 for an easy layup.

DIAGRAM 3: Option 2. If 3 can't get the pass to 4, then he or she should swing the ball over to 2 at the top of the key. 2 looks for 5 coming off 4's screen and cutting toward the basket. If 5 isn't open, 2 looks for 1 doubling back over 4 for a jump shot near the elbow.

SIDELINE DOUBLE STACK

Vinod Vachani,
Welham Girls High School,
Dehra Dun, India

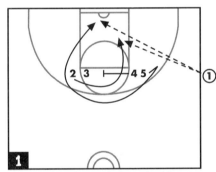

DIAGRAM 1: Break from double stack at the elbow. 5 runs a loop to the basket seeking a pass from 1. 2 follows through the lane, using the screen set up by 4, and looks for the ball.

DIAGRAM 2: If the initial options fail, 3 sets a screen for 5 and 5 rolls toward the basket. Simultaneously, 2 sets a screen for 4 and rolls out to the wing. 1 passes to the open player.

> ## "I'm not against taking shots, but I am against taking bad shots."
>
> *—Hank Iba*

SIDELINE INBOUND FOR POST PLAYER

Brad Duncan,
Fox High School,
Arnold, Mo.

DIAGRAM 1: 3 (your best shooter) comes off 5's screen. 2 sets a screen for 1 (this draws the defender away from the block). 5 rolls and seals his or her defender after screening for 3. The defender guarding 5 often tries to fight through the screen and provide help, making it easy for 5 to seal and gain

position between the defender and the basket. 4 can either throw it to 3 in the corner, hit 5 on the lob or pass to 1 at half court.

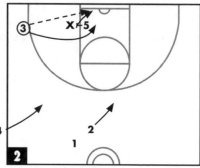

DIAGRAM 2: If 3 gets the inbound pass, he or she can either shoot a quick jump shot or throw an entry pass to 5.

SIDE-OUT (VS. MAN)

Melody Owsley,
Racine Prairie High School,
Racine, Wis.

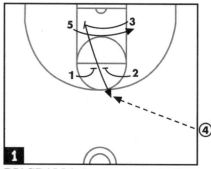

DIAGRAM 1: 3 screens away for 5. 3 then cuts between 1 and 2, who set a double screen. 4 passes the ball to 3.

DIAGRAM 2: 3 reverses the ball to 1 while 2 and 5 set staggered screens for 4. 1 passes to 4 off the back screens.

SIDELINE INBOUND SERIES

Russell Hoffman,
Sanchez High School,
Tamuning, Guam

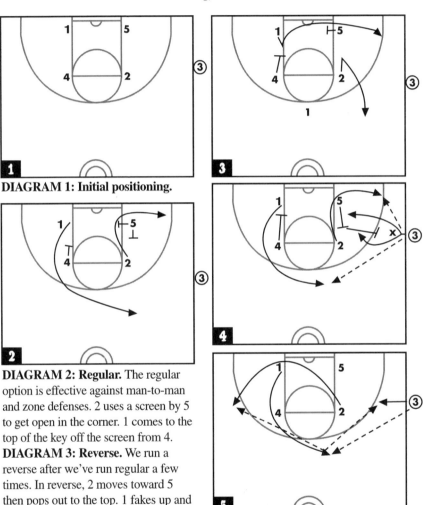

DIAGRAM 1: Initial positioning.

DIAGRAM 2: Regular. The regular option is effective against man-to-man and zone defenses. 2 uses a screen by 5 to get open in the corner. 1 comes to the top of the key off the screen from 4.

DIAGRAM 3: Reverse. We run a reverse after we've run regular a few times. In reverse, 2 moves toward 5 then pops out to the top. 1 fakes up and cuts to the ball side along the baseline off a screen from 5.

DIAGRAM 4: Back Pick. Back pick is used against man-to-man. The action is the same as regular, except after 2 cuts around 5, 5 breaks out and sets a back pick for 3 stepping inbounds.

DIAGRAM 5: Swing. We use swing against a tight zone or sagging man-to-man with post denial and doubling down. Instead of cutting around 5, 2 cuts around to 4's side of the floor and spots up. 3 inbounds to 1. 1 looks to return the pass to 3 or swings it to 2.

SIDELINE OUT-OF-BOUNDS

Marty Gaughan, Head Boys Coach,
Benet Academy,
Lisle, Ill.

DIAGRAM 1: 2 inbounds the ball. 5 and 4 downscreen for 1 and 3 who flash out high to the top.

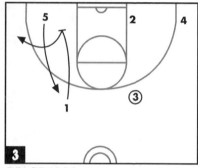

DIAGRAM 3: 1 downscreens for 5 who replaces up top. After setting the screen, 1 fades to the corner.

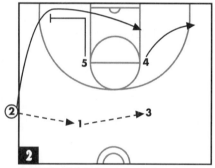

DIAGRAM 2: 2 passes to 1 and cuts all the way to the baseline off 5's screen. 4 flashes to the 3-point area on the weak side. 1 passes to 3.

DIAGRAM 4: 3 passes to 5. 2 pops up and sets a screen for 3 who breaks toward the basket. 4 breaks to the top, replacing 3. 5 passes to 1 for a 3-point shot or hits 3 cutting to the basket.

> *"Some people believe you win with your five best players, but I found out that you win with the five who fit together best."*
>
> —*Red Auerbach*

"HORNET" SIDE OUT-OF-BOUNDS PLAY

Marc Comstock
Emporia State University
Emporia, Kan.

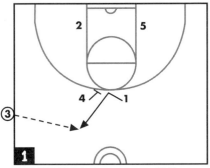

DIAGRAM 1: 1 gets open off 4's screen. 3 passes to 1.

DIAGRAM 2: 1 dribbles to the opposite side and looks for 2 coming off 5's screen for an outside shot, feeds 5 in the mid-post area or lobs the ball in to 4. 3 goes to the block, then back picks 4 and releases for the shot. 4 receives the back pick and cuts to the basket looking for the lob pass. 5 screens for 2 then posts up.

DIAGRAM 3: 1 passes to 3. 2 runs the baseline off screens set by 4 and 5. 3 faces the basket and looks for 2 cutting toward the hoop.

DIAGRAM 4: Dribble Option. 1 passes to 3 and sets staggered screens for 2. 3 dribbles to the opposite side of the floor and passes to either 4 or 2 off the staggered pick. 4 posts up.

SIDE OUT VS. AGGRESSIVE MAN-TO-MAN

DuWayne Krause
Immanuel Lutheran School
Marshfield, Wis.

We often get pressured on our sideline inbounds passes. By spreading out along the sideline, if the defense continues to pressure, they are forced to play 1-on-1 without much help. It also opens up potential drives to the basket.

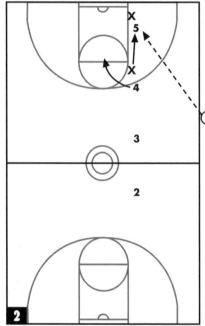

DIAGRAM 2: If the defender on 5 plays behind, pass directly to 5 for a 1-on-1 to the basket. If 4's defender doubles down, 4 can cut to the basket.

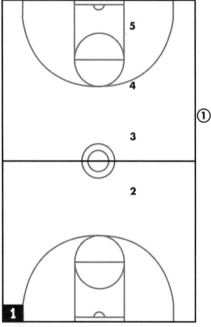

DIAGRAM 1: 1 should be your point guard (and best passer), 5 should be your "go to" player. Stay spread out to isolate the defenders.

> *"Great teamwork is the only way we create the breakthroughs that define our careers."*
>
> —Pat Riley

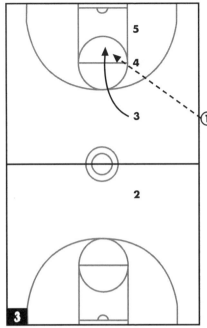

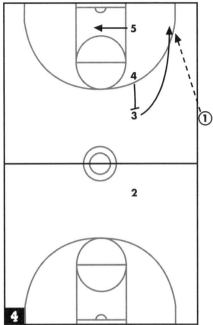

DIAGRAM 3: You can also cut 3 to the basket if the defense is playing tight or fronting.

DIAGRAM 4: The final option has 5 dropping to the basket to take his or her defender deeper in the lane. 4 screens for 3, who cuts to the corner. 3 can shoot, pass to 5 or wait and set up the offense.

"Young athletes, like all young people, must realize that the future holds extraordinary challenges for everyone and they must accept those challenges as part of life. Honesty and integrity are the most important. Never compromise on what you know is right."

—Lenny Wilkens

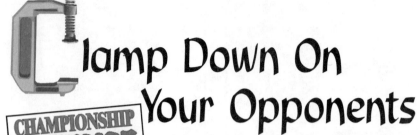

Clamp Down On Your Opponents

CHAMPIONSHIP DEFENSE

Proven Defensive Tactics That Win Games

Regardless of your team's offensive power, your players can compete in every game by playing championship defense.

To develop the critical defensive strategies needed to play at a championship level, check out hundreds of the best defensive tips, techniques and secrets from many of the brightest coaches in basketball with *Championship Defense*!

Featuring rock-solid, in-depth instructional ideas and 238 easy-to-follow diagrams, the 51 outstanding defenses found in this 160-page book include ...

- Full-Court
- Multiple
- Traps
- Man-To-Man
- Zones
- Rotating
- Specialties
- Half-Court
- Thumbs-Down
- Pressure
- Junk Defenses
- End Of Game
- Three-Quarter Court
- Post Double-Team
- Under The Basket
- 3-Point Shot

Every page of *Championship Defense* contains valuable defensive nuggets of knowledge that you'll forge into your own highly personalized defensive program for use at any level of competition.

160 pages......Only $18.95

There's An Old Saying That "Defense Is The Great Equalizer!"
Get Ready To Play Championship Defense By Ordering This Book Today!

Ordering information...

Send your check or credit card information to:
Winning Hoops, P.O. Box 624, Brookfield, WI 53008-0624

FOR FASTER SERVICE
CALL: (800) 645-8455 (U.S. only) **or** (262) 782-4480 • **Fax:** (262) 782-1252
E-mail: info@lesspub.com • **Web site:** www.winninghoops.com

Add $4 for shipping and handling for the 1st book and $1 shipping and handling for each additional book.
Wisconsin residents need to add 5.1 percent sales tax. For Canadian and other foreign shipping, add $8 for the
first book and $5 for each additional book purchased. Payable in U.S. funds drawn on a U.S. bank only.

Priority Code: SCORCH

Chapter 4

QUICK HITTERS

ZONE OFFENSE QUICK HITTER

Glenn Flannigan, Head Coach,
Methven Youth Basketball, Methven, Mass.

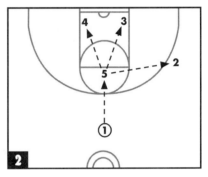

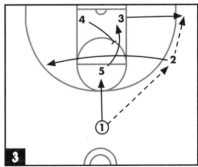

DIAGRAM 1: Initial set. 1 brings the ball up the floor, while 4 and 5 set up staggered on the same side at the low block. 3 is on the opposite block and 2 lines up behind the 3-point line at the free-throw line extended. 5 pops up to the foul line.

DIAGRAM 2: Option A. 1 passes to 5, who turns and faces the basket. 5 has the option to pass to 4 who's curled into the lane or to 3 who's curled into the lane from the opposite block. As a third option, 5 can also look to pass to 2 for a quick 3-pointer.

DIAGRAM 3: Option B. If 5 is covered, 1 passes to 2 and breaks down to the foul line. 2 passes to 3 who's out to the ball-side corner. 4 breaks and sets an upscreen for 5 who comes off the screen and rolls to the basket. 3 can either shoot a baseline 3-pointer, pass to 5 rolling to the basket or hit 1 for a foul-line jumper.

QUICK-HITTING 1-4 HIGH PLAY

Bill Agronin, Head Womens Coach,
Niagara University,
Niagara, N.Y.

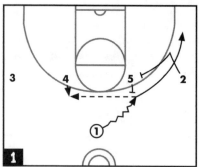

DIAGRAM 1: "Special." 1 dribbles right and passes to 4 popping out to the top. 5 and 2 set staggered screens for 1, who cuts to the corner behind the 3-point line.

DIAGRAM 2: 4 throws a skip pass to either 1 in the corner or 2 rolling to the top. After the pass, 3 sets a screen for 4 and 4 breaks into the corner looking to receive a skip pass for the 3-point shot.

1-4 QUICK HITTER (VS. MAN)

Les Wilson, Head Boys Coach,
Cumberland High School,
Toledo, Ill.

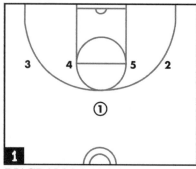

DIAGRAM 1: Initial alignment is out of a 1-4 high set.

DIAGRAM 2: 2 loses the defender by making a V-cut to the basket, then pops back out. 1 passes to 2, while 3 breaks

to the ball-side block.

DIAGRAM 3: 2 can immediately enter the ball in to 3 if 3 has the defender pinned.

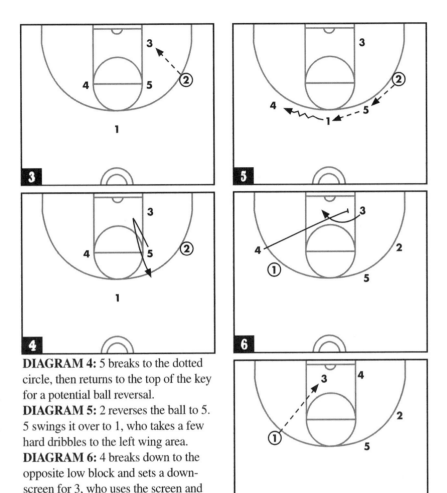

DIAGRAM 4: 5 breaks to the dotted circle, then returns to the top of the key for a potential ball reversal.

DIAGRAM 5: 2 reverses the ball to 5. 5 swings it over to 1, who takes a few hard dribbles to the left wing area.

DIAGRAM 6: 4 breaks down to the opposite low block and sets a down-screen for 3, who uses the screen and rolls across the lane, flashing toward the ball.

DIAGRAM 7: 1 enters the ball to 3 for a good shot opportunity.

"You can't get much done in life if you only work on the days when you feel good."

—*Jerry West*

PICK-AND-ROLL QUICK HITTER

Rick Berger, Former Head Womens Coach,
Westfield State College,
Westfield, Mass.

out to the weak-side wing area. 3 fills 1's spot at the top of the key.

DIAGRAM 1: Option A. 1 has the ball up top, while 3 and 2 line up wide. 5 and 4 are positioned at opposite low blocks. 5 breaks to the top and sets a pick for 1. 1 passes to 2 and uses 5's screen to break toward the hoop. 2 looks to hit 1 cutting through the lane. If the pass isn't there, 1 flashes back

DIAGRAM 2: Option B. 1 passes to 2. 4 breaks up and sets a screen for 2. 2 dribbles around the screen and drives to the hoop. 2 and 4 should look for the give-and-go on the pick-and-roll move.

1-3-1 QUICK HITTER

Bill Agronin, Head Womens Coach,
Niagara University,
Niagara, N.Y.

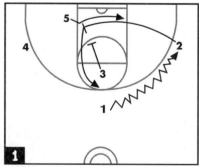

DIAGRAM 1: 1 dribbles toward 2, sending 2 to screen for 5. 3 quickly screens for 2 (screen the screener).

DIAGRAM 2: On the pass from 1 to 2, 4 sets a downscreen for 3. 3 pops out and looks for an open jump shot.

       SCOREBOARD SCORCHERS

DIAGRAM 3: After the pass to 3, 2 downscreens for 5 coming toward the top of the key.

DIAGRAM 4: When 5 receives the pass, 5 can either shoot or pass to 2 coming off a screen from 1.

"CAROLINA"

Rick Berger, Former Head Womens Coach,
Westfield State College,
Westfield, Mass.

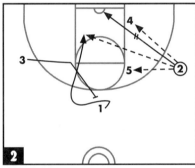

DIAGRAM 1: 1 has the ball up top, while 3 and 2 line up wide. 5 and 4 are positioned at opposite low blocks. 4 slides across the lane and sets a screen for 5. 5 cuts up to the opposite elbow. After setting the screen, 4 rolls back across the lane to his or her initial spot. 1 passes to 2.

DIAGRAM 2: 3 breaks across and sets a screen for 1, who loses his or her defender and rolls off 3's screen and cuts toward the basket.

2 can shoot a 3-pointer, throw an entry pass in to 4 on the low block, pass to 5 in the high post or look to hit 1 streaking toward the basket for a layup.

QUICK HITTER FOR POINT GUARD

Fran Satalin Jr.,
Cazenovia College,
Cazenovia, N.Y

DIAGRAM 1: 1 passes to 3 on the wing and cuts through the lane to the opposite block. 2 diagonal cuts to the ball side block with 5, while 4 rolls to the top and replaces 2.

DIAGRAM 2: As 3 reverses the ball to 4, 2 and 5 cross the lane to set a double screen for 1.

DIAGRAM 3: 4 passes to 1 after he or she clears the double screen.

"FLAT" OUT OF 1-4 LOW SET

Mark Zacher,
Mount Saint Mary's College,
Emmitsburg, Md.

DIAGRAM 1: Run out of a 1-4 low set, 1 enters the ball with a dribble entry to the wing area. On the dribble movement, 4 and 5 both flash high to the elbows. 2 and 3 remain behind the 3-point line in the corners.

DIAGRAM 2: 3 cuts diagonally through to the lane and sets a screen for 4. 4 cuts hard off the screen and posts up on the ball-side block. This cross

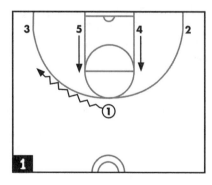

screen should result in a good shot, particularly if the defenders switch.

DIAGRAM 3: If the first scoring option isn't there, 3 and 5 set a stag-gered double screen for the weak-side guard (2) who flashes high looking for a pass from 1 and a quick shot.

"14"

Bill Agronin, Head Womens Coach,
Niagara University,
Niagara, N.Y.

DIAGRAM 1: Out of a 1-4 high set, 1 dribbles right and throws a pass left to 5 popping out to the top of the key. 2 breaks hard to the low-block on the weak side.

DIAGRAM 2: 5 passes back to 1 on the right wing area. On the pass, 2 breaks up high across the lane and sets a screen for 5. 5 uses 2's screen and rolls hard to the basket. 4 slides down and screens 2, who uses the screen and rolls to the top of the key.

1 looks to hit 5 rolling to the basket or hits 2 for a 3-point shot. If neither shot option is available, then 1 passes to 2, where 2 and 4 will run a pick-and-roll action.

"ANGLE" BOX-SET QUICK HITTER

Brad McGhee, Head Boys Coach,
Liberty High School
Mountain View, Mo.

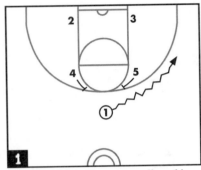

DIAGRAM 1: Players are aligned in a box-set formation with 4 and 5 lined up at the elbows, while 2 and 3 are positioned on opposite low blocks. 1 has the ball at the top and dribbles off a screen set by 4 or 5.

DIAGRAM 3: If 2 wasn't open for the 3-point shot, 1 keeps the ball. After 5's screen, 3 sets a cross screen for 5 who breaks across the lane and sets up on the ball-side block. 1 looks for 5 for a post-up shot.

DIAGRAM 2: 5 immediately screens down for 2, who comes off the screen and goes to the top. If 2 is wide open, 1 passes to 2 for a 3-pointer.

DIAGRAM 4: If 5 isn't open, 3 comes to the top off a double screen set by 2 and 4 and looks for the 3-point shot. 1 passes to 3 for a 3-pointer or looks to get the ball into 5 who's posting up on the low block.

"OKEMOS"

Mike Ingram, Head Mens Coach,
Lansing Community College,
Lansing, Mich.

In this series of quick-hitting plays, 1 should be your point guard, 2 is your best 3-point shooter and 3 is your best inside scorer cutting to the basket. 4 and 5 are both post players who can rebound.

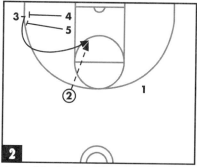

toward the basket. 2 hits 3 curling into the lane.

DIAGRAM 1: First Option. 1 dribbles toward 3 to start the play. 3 runs the baseline to the opposite corner. 4 and 5 both break down to the weak-side low block and set a double screen for 2. 2 comes hard off the downscreen and pops out top behind the 3-point line. 1 passes to 2 for a quick 3-point shot.

DIAGRAM 2: Second Option. If 2 doesn't have an open look for a 3-point shot, then 4 and 5 break out to the corner and set a double screen for 3, who uses the screen and curls into the lane,

DIAGRAM 3: Third Option. This play is run out of the same set as Option 1, only this time, when the double screen is set, 5 reverses back and rolls to the basket.

1 fakes a pass to 2 and hits 5 flashing to the basket.

> *"The main ingredient of stardom is the rest of the team."*
>
> *—John Wooden*

QUICK-HIT SET PLAY

Nate Webber, Head Boys Coach,
McCorristin Catholic, High School
Trenton, N.J.

DIAGRAM 1: 1 dribbles to the side of the floor where the shooting guard is positioned. 2 cross screens for 5.

DIAGRAM 2: If 5 isn't open, 3 and 4 set a double screen for 2 to come out to the top of the key for a shot.

QUICK SHOT

Jayme Jones,
Valley Springs High School
Valley Springs, Ark.

DIAGRAM 1: This play is run from a box set with 4 and 5 on opposite elbows, while 1 has the ball on top. 2 and 3 set up on opposite low blocks.

1 makes a dribble entry to either side of the floor (to the right in this Diagram). 2 breaks up through the lane and comes off a triple screen set by 3, 4 and

5. 1 gets to the wing area and throws a pass back to 2 at the top of the key.

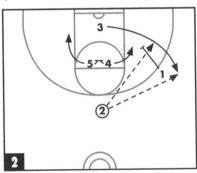

DIAGRAM 2: After setting the screen for 2 in the lane, 3 pops out to the right wing area, coming off a downscreen set by 1. 2 passes to 3 for a quick 2- or 3-point shot.

SCOREBOARD SCORCHERS

Chapter 5

LAST-SECOND GAME WINNERS

"POPCORN" LAST-SHOT PLAY (VS. MAN)

Wayne Walters, Head Mens Coach,
Thaddeus Stevens Technical College,
Lancaster, Pa.

For the following play, the numbered players can be any player you wish and aren't representative of the player's position.

DIAGRAM 1: Option 1. 3 and 5 line up wide in the corners on the baseline, while 1 has the ball out top. 4 and 2 pop up and set a screen for 1 on either side.

1 reads the defense and decides which screen he or she will use (in this case 4's screen). 1 dribbles off 4's screen and drives to the basket. If 4's defender drops down to switch, 1 and 4 will run a pick-and-roll action.

DIAGRAM 2: Option 2. 2 and 4 pop up and set screens for 1 on either side.

1 reads the defense and decides which way he or she will run the play (in this case 4's screen). 1 dribbles off 4's screen and drives to the hoop. If 3's defender slides over to deny penetration, then 1 can kick it to 3 in the corner for an open 3-point shot. 2 replaces 1 up top.

5 steps in and sets a screen for 1 on the baseline. 1 curls around the screen and breaks up to the weak-side wing. If 3 doesn't get an open look at a 3-pointer, he or she passes back out to 2 on top and 2 swings the ball over to 1 for a jump shot on the wing. 2 can also look for 5 stepping into the lane and rolling to the hoop.

LAST-SECOND PLAY (SIDE OUT-OF-BOUNDS)

Alan McAughtry,
Waverley Falcons,
Melbourne, Australia

DIAGRAM 1: 2 takes the ball out on the side. 4 and 3 set a double screen for 1. 5 posts up on the ball-side block. 1 comes off the double screen and breaks toward the ball. 2 quickly looks to throw the ball to 5 in the post, then passes to 1.

DIAGRAM 2: 1 looks to hit 5 in the post (A), while 3 and 4 break out to the perimeter. If 5 isn't open, 1 passes to 3 (A) who quickly swings it over to 4 (B). While the ball is moving around the perimeter, 2 breaks to the basket and runs to the opposite block. 4 hits 2 (C) for a scoring opportunity.

LAST-SECOND SHOT (VS. MAN)

Kenneth Adams, Retired Basketball Coach,
Temple, Ga.

point line. After setting the screen, 3 will reverse and go to the ball-side corner.

DIAGRAM 1: 2 brings the ball into play. 3 sets a screen across the lane for 4 who cuts to the ball side behind the 3-

DIAGRAM 2: 2 passes to 4 at the

wing and follows the pass, looking for a hand off or return pass back from 4. 1 follows 2 and sets a screen for 4. 5 breaks to the corner and sets a baseline screen for 3.

DIAGRAM 3: After handing the ball off to 2, 4 rolls off 1's screen and breaks hard toward the basket. At the same time, 3 uses 5's screen and also breaks hard to the basket. 2 passes to either 3 or 4 rolling to the basket.

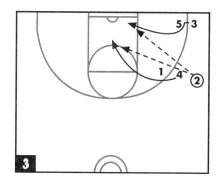

END-OF-GAME SPECIAL

Rick Berger, Former Head Womens Coach,
Westfield State College,
Westfield, Mass.

DIAGRAM 1: 2 starts out of bounds and acts like he or she will be the inbounder. 4 cuts hard out of bounds and 2 throws a lateral pass to 4. 5 steps up and sets a screen for 2 who streaks upcourt on the right side. At the same time as 2 streaks upcourt, 1 curls to the opposite side of the court and comes off a screen set by 3.

4's first option is to hit 2 with a baseball pass as 2 streaks upcourt. If 2 isn't open, then 4 inbounds to 1 who dribbles hard down the left side of the court and tries to take it all the way.

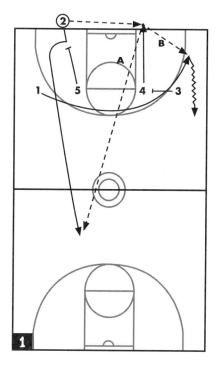

DOUBLE-STRONG SERIES:
LAST SHOT (VS. MAN OR ZONE)

Wayne Walters, Head Mens Coach,
Thaddeus Stevens Technical College,
Lancaster, Pa.

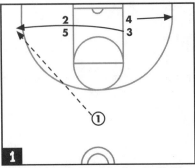

DIAGRAM 1: Double-Strong Dribble Option (A). 1 has the ball on top while 2 and 5 form a double stack on the left-side low block. 3 and 4 form a double stack on the right-side low block. 3 breaks hard to the left side of the floor, while 4 pops out behind the 3-point line on the right. 1 passes to 3.

DIAGRAM 2: Double-Strong Dribble Option (B). 2 curls around a screen set by 5 and pops up behind the 3-point line on the ball-side. 1 slides over behind the 3-point line on the weak side.

3 takes a few hard dribbles in to draw the defense, then has the option

to shoot, pass to 2, pass to 1 or throw a cross-court pass to 4 for a shot.

DIAGRAM 3: Double-Strong Dribble Option (C). If the ball goes cross court to either 1 or 4. They should look for 5 sliding across the lane, into either the low or high post.

DIAGRAM 4: Double-Strong Crossover Option (A). In this set, after 3 and 4 make their initial cuts wide to each side of the floor (see Diagram 1), 1 can dribble entry to the left, then makes a crossover pass to 4 in the corner.
DIAGRAM 5: Double-Strong Crossover Option (B). After the pass to 4, 5 cuts hard to the ball side behind

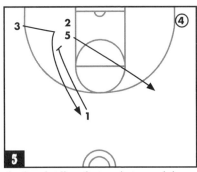

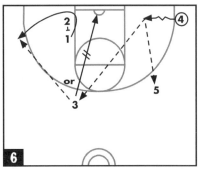

the 3-point line. 3 steps in toward the low block and then comes off a down-screen set by 1.

DIAGRAM 6: Double-Strong Crossover Option (C). 2 sets a screen for 1 who curls around the screen and fades into the weak-side corner behind

the 3-point line. 4 takes a few hard dribbles in to draw the defense, then looks to hit either 5 or 3 with a pass. If the pass goes to 3, he or she can either shoot a 3-pointer or immediately swing the ball to 1 in the corner for a game-winning 3-pointer.

4-SECOND WINNER

Michael Ortiz,
Western Samar, Philippines

DIAGRAM 1: 2 sets a screen for 3. 2 uses a screen set by 1. 1 makes a V-cut downcourt and comes back to receive the inbound pass from 5.

1 pushes the ball downcourt and looks for 3 for the jump shot. 3 and 2 interchange from one side to the other.

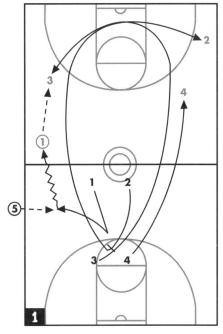

END-OF-GAME, FULL-COURT INBOUND

Pat Sullivan, Head Mens Coach,
University of St. Francis,
Joliet, Ill.

DIAGRAM 1: This is a great play to run if there are only 5 or 10 seconds left in the game. Both 3 and 5 fake toward the ball then break downcourt and spot up behind the 3-point line on opposite sides of the floor

1 screens for 5 and seals. Because the defense will often switch on this, 4 can hit 1 who then has the middle third of the floor open. 1 quickly advances the ball looking for a shot or passes to 2 or 3.

If the defense doesn't switch and 1 is fronted, then 4 passes to 5. 5 looks to hit 1 and 1 advances the ball quickly downcourt.

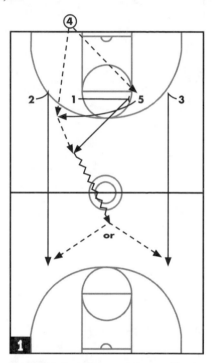

3 PLAYERS IN A STACK (LAST SHOT)

Willie J. Banks,
Dunbar Vocational High School
Chicago, Ill.

DIAGRAM 1: Your best jumper should be the player in the 5 position. 5 pops up to the free-throw line as 1 dribbles toward 2. 2 breaks to the deep corner.
DIAGRAM 2: When 1 is at the free-throw line extended, 3 and 4 both set a back screen for 5. 5 breaks to the hoop, looking for the lob pass.
DIAGRAM 3: If 5 can't score off the

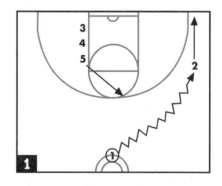

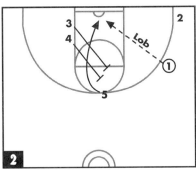

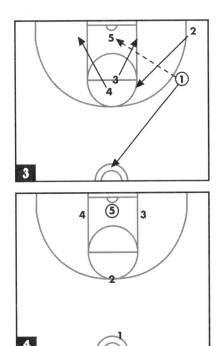

lob, he or she must — at the very least — catch the ball and try to go back up for the score.

DIAGRAM 4: The triangle positioning shown here must be set after every shot to maintain defensive balance on any missed shots or transition opportunities by your opponent.

"HARVARD" LAST-SECOND INBOUND PLAY

Pat Sullivan, Head Mens Coach,
University of St. Francis,
Joliet, Ill.

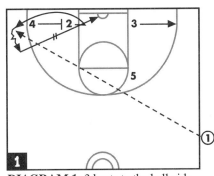

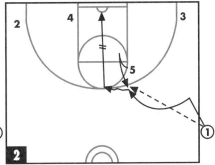

DIAGRAM 1: 3 busts to the ball-side corner. 4 screens 2's defender and 2 goes out for the 3-point shot. 1 makes a baseball pass to 2. 3 and 5 double-team the weak-side rebound.

DIAGRAM 2: If 1 can't pass to 2, then 5 fakes to the basket and comes to the ball looking to straddle the 3-point line. 1 hits 5, tries to run the defender down toward the basket and rubs off 5 for the handoff and 3-point shot.

"HOME-RUN" GAME WINNER

Tom Jicha, Basketball Coach,
Miami Sunset Senior High School,
Miami, Fla.

This is a great full-court inbounds play to run when there are less than 5 seconds remaining and the opponent has just scored.

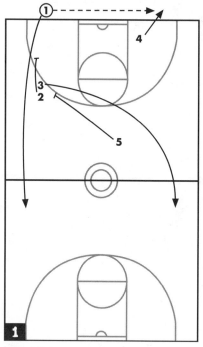

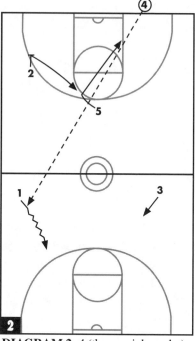

DIAGRAM 1: While 1 is the inbounder, 4 steps out across the baseline and 1 passes laterally to 4. 5 screens for 3 who heads up the left side. 2 screens for 1 who comes inbound and streaks down the right side of the court.

DIAGRAM 2: 4 (the new inbounder) fakes a pass to 3 on the left side, but then makes a baseball pass to 1 streaking downcourt for a great scoring opportunity.

The key to making this play successful is for 4 to look at 3 the whole time to try to get the back defenders to commit a few steps toward 3's direction.

"WISHBONE" BUZZER BEATER

Tom Jicha, Basketball Coach,
Miami Sunset Senior High School,
Miami, Fla.

This play is used when there is less than 5 seconds left and you can't run the baseline.

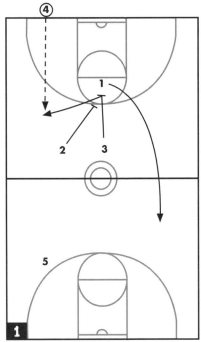

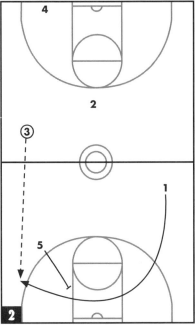

DIAGRAM 1: 5 lines up deep. 3 screens for 1 who curls around the screen and flies up the left side of the floor. 2 executes screen-the-screener action for 3, who comes off the screen and receives the inbound pass from 4.

DIAGRAM 2: 1 continues streaking down the floor and curls along the baseline, coming off a downscreen set by 5 at the low post. 1 curls into the corner behind the 3-point line and receives a pass from 3. 1 can either shoot the 3-pointer or dump it down to 5 in the low post for a shot.

> *"My advice to kids?*
> *Don't be like me — be better than me."*
>
> —Shaquille O'Neal

FULL-COURT GAME WINNERS

Lason Perkins, Former Coach,
Cary High School,
Cary N.C.

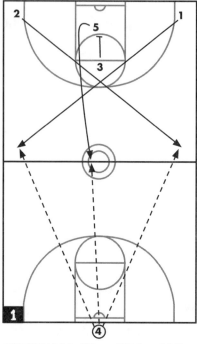

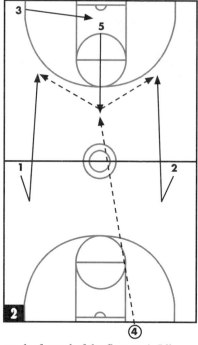

DIAGRAM 1: "Deep-X." 1 and 2 line up in the far corners at the opposite end of the floor to the inbounder. 3 and 5 are lined up in the lane on the far end of the floor. 4 inbounds the bound.

When the official hands 4 the ball, 3 sets a screen for 5 going to the ball. 1 and 2 cut diagonally toward midcourt. 4 passes to the open player.

DIAGRAM 2: "Home Run." 4 inbounds the ball, while 1 and 2 are lined up at midcourt on opposite side-lines. 3 lines up in the opposite corner

on the far end of the floor to 4. 5 lines up in the lane on the opposite side just in front of the basket.

When the official hands the ball to 4, 1, 2 and 5 all break toward the ball. 4 throws a baseball pass to 5 at the opposite 3-point arc. As the ball is in the air, 1 and 2 break back toward the basket looking for a quick catch-and-pass by 5. 5 hits either 1 or 2 for a quick jump shot (2- or 3-pointer) while 3 crashes the boards looking for an offensive put back.

"DUKE" (VS. MAN)

Wayne Walters, Head Mens Coach,
Thaddeus Stevens Technical College,
Lancaster, Pa.

This is an outstanding last-second play with multiple options. The numbered players can be any player you wish and aren't representative of the player's position.

In the initial set, 1 has the ball up top, while 2 and 3 sets up a stack on the left-side low block. 4 and 5 set up a stack on the elbow at the right side.

DIAGRAM 1: Option 1 (Dribble Toward The High Stack). 1 dribbles to the right side, while 4 and 5 criss-cross with 5 rolling to the hoop and 4 popping to the top of the key. 2 breaks out to the weak-side wing area behind the 3-point line and 3 breaks along the baseline and cuts to the ball-side corner behind the 3-point line.

On the drive, 1 looks to hit 5 rolling to the hoop, 3 in the corner for a 3-pointer or throws a kick-out pass over to 2 on the opposite side of the floor for a 3-point shot.

DIAGRAM 2: Option 2 (Dribble Toward The Low Stack). While 1 dribbles toward the left side, 4 breaks across the lane and goes to the ball-side corner behind the 3-point line. 2

sets a downscreen for 3 who rolls around the screen and pops behind the 3-point line on the ball side. 5 breaks to the weak-side wing area behind the 3-point line.

1 passes to 4, who can either shoot a 3-pointer, hit 3 for a 3-point shot or swing a cross-court pass over to 5 on the opposite side of the floor for a quick 3-pointer.

DIAGRAM 3: Option 2 (Continued). If the cross-court pass is too dangerous or it can't be made, you can have 4 pass to 3 and 3 quickly swings the ball back out to 1 on top. 1 can dribble drive, draw the defense and kick it out to 5 for a 3-point shot.

1-4 LOW LAST-SHOT ATTEMPT

Alan McAughtry,
Waverley Falcons,
Melbourne, Australia

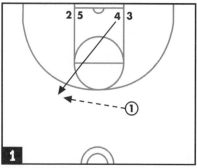

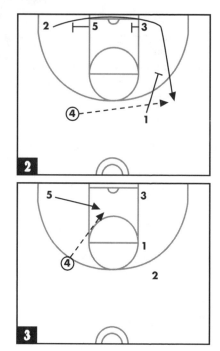

DIAGRAM 1: Line up flat on the baseline. When 1 signals, 4 cuts opposite and sets up outside the 3-point line.

DIAGRAM 2: At the same time, 2 cuts along staggered baseline screens by 5 and 3, cutting to the 3-point line for a pass from 4. 1 can step down and screen for 2 if a defender has cheated.

DIAGRAM 3: As soon as 4 receives the pass from 1, 5 steps into the lane, looking for a pass from 4 and a post-up shot in the lane.

This play works extremely well if it's used when the opposition is in foul trouble, especially the opposing post players.

> *"Some criticism will be honest, some won't.*
> *Some praise you will deserve, some you won't.*
> *You can't let praise or criticism get to you.*
> *It's a weakness to get caught up in either one."*
>
> —John Wooden

Chapter 6

PLAYS VS. MAN-TO-MAN DEFENSE

LOB PLAY (VS. MAN)

Keith Cooper, Assistant Mens Coach,
Central Washington University,
Ellensburg, Wash.

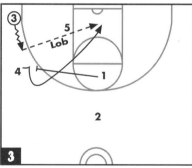

DIAGRAM 1: 4 pops out to the wing area and receives the pass from 1. 3 cuts to the corner off 5's baseline screen.

DIAGRAM 2: 4 passes to 3 in the corner. 5 posts up on the ball-side block. 1 sets a downscreen for 2. 2 pops to the top of the key area.

DIAGRAM 3: 4 V-cuts and uses a screen by 1 to break toward the basket looking for a lob pass. 3 dribbles toward the screen to create the proper timing and throws the lob pass to 4.

"DUO" SET PLAY (VS. MAN)

Rhonda Farney, Head Girls Coach,
And Kellye Richardson, Assistant Girls Coach,
Georgetown High School,
Georgetown, Texas

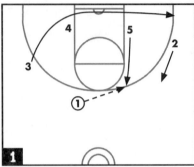

DIAGRAM 1: 4 and 5 set up on opposite low blocks while 2 and 3 line up wide on the wings. 1 has the ball on top. 5 cuts up and receives a pass from 1. 3 cuts to the basket along the baseline and winds up in the ball-side corner behind the 3-point line. 2 pops up top toward 5.

DIAGRAM 2: 1 cuts to the weak-side corner. 4 flashes up hard to set a screen for 5, who rolls around 4's screen and drives to the basket. 4 and 5 run a pick-and-roll action in the paint. If the defense collapses, they should look to throw it into either corner for a 3-point shot by 1 or 3.

"TORNADO" (VS. MAN)

John Farruggio,
Wall, N.J.

DIAGRAM 1: Space the court so that the middle is clear. 1 and 2 should be

good ball handlers. 3 should be a good slasher. 1 dribbles toward 2's side.

DIAGRAM 2: 5 pops out to the corner. 4 upscreens for 3. 3 comes off 4's screen and slashes to the lane. 2 V-cuts sharply and pops out to receive the pass from 1. 2 can shoot, penetrate or look to 3 cutting to the basket.

DIAGRAM 3: After you run this play a few times, the defense will make adjustments. 4 upscreens for 3 who breaks toward the lane. But this time, 3 runs all the way through to the baseline

and to the opposite corner and sets a screen for 5. 5 comes off 4's screen and breaks toward the basket or can

pop up toward the elbow looking for pass. 1 can hit 5 or pass to 2.

"EASTERN" (VS. MAN)

Chris Kusnerick,
St. Anthony High School,
Effingham, Ill.

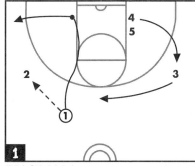

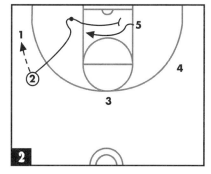

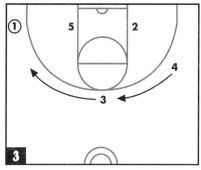

DIAGRAM 1: 1 passes to 2 on the wing. After the pass, 1 cuts to the basket and posts up on the block or breaks to the corner. 3 cuts to the top of the key. 4 replaces 3.

DIAGRAM 2: 2 passes to 1 in the corner then breaks to the block for the post up. If 2 isn't open, he or she slides across the lane and sets a cross screen for 5 cutting along the baseline toward the ball.

DIAGRAM 3: 3 replaces 2 and 4 replaces 3 at the top of the key.

TWO-HIGH, MAN-TO-MAN OFFENSE

Keith Siefkes,
Beth Eden Baptist School,
Denver, Colo.

DIAGRAM 1: 2 dribble enters to the right side. 5 sets up at the foul line, while 4 lines up at the right elbow. In the event that 2 can't go right, he or she dribbles left and 4 moves to the left elbow.

DIAGRAM 2: 2 dribbles to the right wing area, while 1 breaks down and cuts off a double screen set by 4 and 5. 5 follows 1 and goes to the ball-side mid-post area. 3 replaces 1 at the point and sets up for the ball reversal. 4 replaces 3. 2 looks to pass to 1 or 5.

DIAGRAM 3: 2 passes to 3, who quickly reverses the ball with a pass to 4. When 4 has the ball, 2 uses 1 and 5 for a double screen and cuts across the lane either under or over the top of the screen, depending on where the defense is playing. 5 follows 1 and sets up in the high post. 4 looks for 2 or 5 coming off the screen. 3 replaces 1.

DIAGRAM 4: 4 now has the ball on the left side. The motion pattern continues in a similar manner as before. 5 is the only player who stays in the same position. Everyone else changes positions based on where they end up after the motion.

"FALCONS" (VS. MAN)

Alan McAughtry, Boys Basketball Coach,
Waverley Falcons,
Melbourne, Australia

This play is run from regular flex-offense positions.

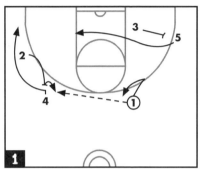

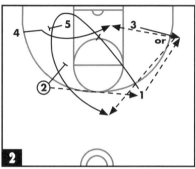

DIAGRAM 1: 2 sets an upscreen for 4, who uses the screen and slides into the corner. 3 sets a back screen for 5 who runs through the lane to the opposite low post. 1 passes to 2 and 2 looks to 5 flashing through the lane or for the quick post-up shot on the low block. 1 fakes a downscreen for 3, but then jumps back out top.

DIAGRAM 2: If 5 wasn't open to receive the initial pass, then 2 passes the ball back to 1, who quickly reverses it to 3 in the corner. After swinging the ball, 1 breaks hard to the basket, stopping briefly in the middle of the lane to set a screen for 4 rolling to the ball-side block. 3 looks to hit 4 in the low post or passes it out top to 1 coming off staggered screens set by 5 and 2 for an open jump shot at the top. 1 should also look for 5 rolling back into the middle of the lane after setting the screen.

If neither of these options gets you a shot, note that you are automatically back into the flex entry and you can run the same play from the other side.

At any time during this play, 1 can break down the defense with dribble penetration and look to drive to the hoop for a good shot.

"WILDCAT" (VS. MAN)

John Kimble, Former Head Boys Coach,
Crestview High School,
Crestview, Fla.

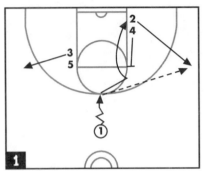

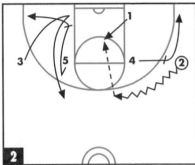

DIAGRAM 1: When 1 dribbles to the top of the key, 2 and 3 pop out to the wings at the free-throw line extended. 4 breaks up to the elbow. 1 passes to either wing and scrapes off the high post pick and posts up on the block.

DIAGRAM 2: If 1 isn't open, 4 ball screens for 2 and then breaks toward the corner. 3 breaks to the block, then pops out top off 5's downscreen. 5 goes to the weak-side corner. The defense should now be spread and 2 can pass to 1 breaking into the lane for an isolation play.

"BLUE DEVIL" MAN OFFENSE

Mark Zacher, Assistant Womens Coach,
Mount Saint Mary College,
Emmitsburg, Md.

This man offense from a 1-4 high set, makes use of the UCLA cut, a shuffle cut and a staggered double screen for scoring options.

DIAGRAM 1: From the 1-4 high set, the ball is entered to either wing on the pass from 1. After making the pass, 1 makes a UCLA cut off the ball-side high post. 2 looks for 1 on the cut.

DIAGRAM 2: After 1 makes the UCLA cut, the weak-side post player (5) steps out top for the ball reversal and swings the ball to 3 on the wing. 2

makes a shuffle cut off 4 and goes to the ball-side box. 3 looks for 2 in the low post.

DIAGRAM 3: After 2 gets to the low post, 4 and 5 break down and set a staggered screen for 1 popping back out to the top of the key. 3 looks to hit 1 for a quick catch-and-shoot opportunity.

"KNICKS" (VS. MAN)

Lason Perkins, Former Coach,
Cary High School,
Cary, N.C.

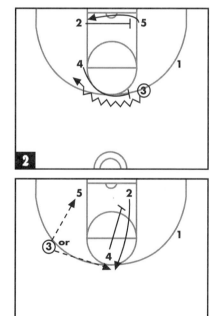

DIAGRAM 1: 1 dribbles to the right side as 5 screens down for 3, who pops up to the ball-side elbow. 1 passes to 3.

DIAGRAM 2: 4 sets a ball screen for 3, while 2 screens across for 5. 5 posts up on the opposite low block. 3 uses 4's screen and dribbles over the top and to the left side of the floor.

DIAGRAM 3: 3 looks to pass to 5 posting up or 2 coming to the top off a screen set by 4 in the lane.

"LASSO" OR "ROMEO" SET PLAY (VS. MAN)

Rhonda Farney, Head Girls Coach,
And Kellye Richardson, Assistant Girls Coach,
Georgetown High School,
Georgetown, Texas

The following play is called "Lasso" when you run it to the left side and "Romeo" when run to the right.

low blocks, but both players cut up to the elbows at the same time. 1 passes to 5 on the left ("Lasso").

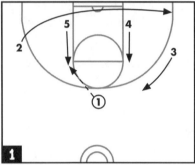

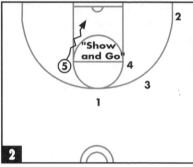

DIAGRAM 1: 1 has the ball up top. 2 cuts along the baseline and into the corner on the far side, while 3 cuts to the top. 4 and 5 start out on opposite

DIAGRAM 2: 5 runs a "show-and-go," where he or she fakes a ball-reversal pass to the overloaded side and then drives to the basket for the shot.

"BAMA" SET PLAY (VS. MAN)

Doug Hughes, Basketball Coach,
Saint Henry, Ohio

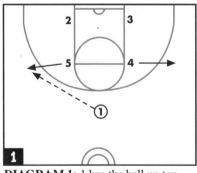

block. 4 and 5 break wide to the wing on each side of the floor. 1 passes to 5.

DIAGRAM 1: 1 has the ball up top with 4 and 5 lined up at opposite elbows. 2 and 3 line up on each low

DIAGRAM 2: 2 and 3 set staggered

screens for 4, who uses both screens and cuts to the basket on the ball side.
DIAGRAM 3: 3 curls around and 1 breaks down into the lane and both players set a double screen for 2. 2 uses the screens and pops to the top of the key. 5 looks to hit 2 for a quick 3-point shot. *Note:* For this play to work, 3 is the key screener and must be quick in getting into position to set the screen for 2.

SIDE OUT-OF-BOUNDS (VS. MAN)

Pete Flotlin,
Billings Central Catholic High School,
Billings, Mont.

This play works well against a man-to-man defense because it doesn't matter how the defenders line up against your best shooter and post-up players.

behind, they may be open for scoring opportunities.

DIAGRAM 1: 1 inbounds the ball, while 3 (your best 3-point shooter) and 5 (your best post player) form a ball-side stack near the high post. 3 breaks into the corner and 5 slides to the mid-post area. If 3 and 5's defenders play

DIAGRAM 2: 4 sets a screen for 2, who V-cuts, uses the screen and breaks toward the ball to receive a pass from 1. 3 and 5 set a staggered screen for 1 who uses the screen and breaks to the opposite high-post area. 2 can either go 1-on-1 or throw a skip pass to 4 who looks for 1 coming across the lane.

MAN-TO-MAN SPECIAL

Marty Gaughan, Head Boys Coach,
Benet Academy,
Lisle, Ill.

This play can be used when you are looking for an inside post up, a back-door lob or a perimeter jump shot.

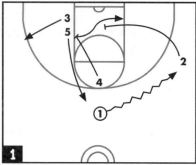

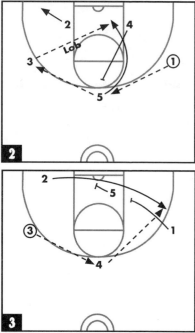

DIAGRAM 1: 1 has the ball and dribbles to the right. 4 sets a downscreen for 5 who pops up to the top of the key. 2 screens the screener by breaking to the middle of the lane and sets a screen for 4, who rolls down to the strong-side low block. 3 releases to the wing on the weak side.

DIAGRAM 2: After setting the screen for 5, 2 fades down to the weak-side low post. 1 passes to 5 who swings the ball quickly over to 3. As the ball is being reversed, 4 breaks up and sets an upscreen for 5. 5 uses the screen and rolls hard toward the basket. 3 looks for 5 on the lob pass.

DIAGRAM 3: If the lob isn't there, 2 rolls back along the baseline off staggered screens set by 5 and 1. 3 passes to 4 and 4 quickly reverses the ball to 2 for a quick catch-and-shoot jumper coming off the staggered screens.

> *"The key to any game is to use your strengths and hide your weaknesses."*
>
> —Paul Westphal

"MICHIGAN" (VS. MAN)

Greg Zeller,
Concord High School,
Concord, Mich.

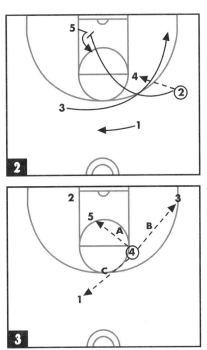

DIAGRAM 1: 1 dribbles to right. 2 flashes to the wing. 1 passes to 2. 4 flashes to the ball-side elbow. 5 replaces 4 and 3 breaks out beyond the 3-point arc.

DIAGRAM 2: 2 passes to 4, then follows the pass and cuts down to the opposite block to screen for 5. 3 follows 2's cut and breaks out to the corner.

DIAGRAM 3: 4's options are:

   A. 5 coming off 2's screen.
   B. 3 in the corner.
   C. 1 for the 3-point shot. If there's no open shot, 1 may restart the offense.

Note: 5 will be open often and can receive a low bounce pass from 4.

This is very effective against a man-to-man that chases instead of switches.

> *"Ball handling is the*
> *backbone of good teamwork."*
>
> —*Pete Maravich*

BOX-SET PLAYS (VS. MAN)

Mack McCarthy, Former Head Coach,
Virginia Commonwealth University,
Richmond, Va.

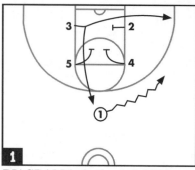

DIAGRAM 1: Option 1. 1 dribbles to the right side, while 5 and 4 set a double screen for 3 just below the foul line. 2 slides over into the lane and sets a screen for 3. 3 reads the defense and uses the screen that he or she feels will get the best open look and comes hard off the screen, looking for a pass from 1 and a quick shot.

DIAGRAM 2: Option 2. 1 dribbles to the right while 2 cuts along the baseline and curls up behind the 3-point line on the weak side. 4 replaces 2 on the low block, while 5 pops to the top and replaces 1.

DIAGRAM 3: Option 2 (Continued). 3 sets a cross screen in the lane for 4, who uses the screen and posts up on

the weak-side low block. 1 passes to 5 on top and 5 quickly swings the ball over to 2.

2 can either shoot a quick 3-point shot or dump it down low to 4 for a post-up scoring opportunity.

"It doesn't matter who scores the points. It's who gets the ball to the scorer."

—Larry Bird

TRIANGLE BASELINE (VS. MAN)

Allen Gainer,
Jefferson Davis Community College,
Brewton, Ala.

DIAGRAM 1: This is an effective, multi-option addition to a triangle offense. 1 passes to 3 and shallow cuts to the right corner. 5 dives to the ball-side post and 2 slides over for reversal.

DIAGRAM 2: 3 makes a baseline pass to 1 and cuts all the way through the lane. 3 keys 5 to set a ball screen for 1.

2 stays at the top of the key and 4 remains above the weak-side wing area.

DIAGRAM 3: While 5 sets a ball screen for 1, 4 simultaneously sets a flare screen for 2. 1 looks to either score, dish off to 5 on a roll or kicks the ball to 2 for a 3-point shot.

Now That Your Playbook Is Loaded, It's Time To Fire Up Your Base Offense...

Zone Busters *(16 pages)* $7.95

A tight zone defense can pose serious headaches for your offense! This detailed 16-page report is loaded with some of the best zone offenses designed to thwart the trickiest of zone defenses. Packed with over a dozen innovative articles and 87 clearly drawn diagrams, *Zone Busters* delivers practical, ready-to-use zone offenses that you can immediately put to work in your program. Bust those tough zone defenses today!

Motion Offense *(16 pages)* $7.95

Nothing will get your team high-percentage scoring opportunities like a solid motion offense. This 16-page Special Coaching Report offers a detailed look at a wide variety of motion offenses that act as weapons against any defense. Every page is loaded with offensive series, set plays, fundamental concepts of motion offense and explanations of how motion works against any defense. This report is the complete guide to continuity offense! All articles are adaptable to every level and easy to put to immediate use with your team.

Triangle Offense *(16 pages)* $7.95

Learn why many coaches are testifying that solid triangle offenses will help you win more games. This 16-page look at the triangle offense sheds new light on its versatility and why defenses are having such a difficult time stopping it! See how different triangle offenses can be run against many different looks and from almost any spot on the floor. Written by some of the world's top experts on triangle offenses, this report will be a new weapon for your team's offense. It's loaded with easy-to-follow diagrams and set plays that are good for every level of competition. This is a must-have offensive report!

To Order, Mail To:

Winning Hoops • P.O. Box 624 • Brookfield, WI 53008-0624

For Faster Service In The U.S., Call: (800) 645-8455 Or (262) 782-4480

Fax: (262) 782-1252 • **E-mail:** info@lesspub.com

Web site: www.winninghoops.com

with credit card information.

Special Coaching Reports ship FREE for U.S. and Canadian orders.

Please add $2.50 for foreign shipments for each report.

Wisconsin residents need to add 5.1 percent sales tax.

Payable in U.S. Funds drawn on a U.S. bank only.

Priority Code: SCORCH

Chapter 7

PLAYS VS. ZONE DEFENSE

ZONE OFFENSE

Glenn Flannigan, Head Coach,
Methven Youth Basketball,
Methven, Mass.

This play works best against a 2-3 zone defense. With all your players having the green light to take the open shot, it opens up the zone for your cutters. The play can be run to either side, but 2 must switch to the strong side.

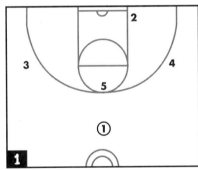

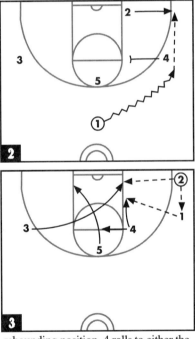

DIAGRAM 1: In the initial alignment, 1 has the ball up top, 5 is positioned at the top of the key, 2 is on the right low block and 3 and 4 line up wide on the wings behind the 3-point line.

DIAGRAM 2: 1 dribbles to the right. 4 breaks in to the ball-side elbow and sets a screen on the top zone defender on that side. 2 pops out to the corner behind the 3-point line. 1 passes to 2 in the corner.

DIAGRAM 3: 5 breaks down to the weak-side low block and sets up in good rebounding position. 4 rolls to either the middle of the free-throw line or cuts down to the ball-side low block. 3 cuts hard across the lane toward the ball.

2 can either shoot, hit 3 cutting across the lane or kick it back out to 1. 1 looks to hit 4 rolling to the basket or shoots a 3-pointer.

PLAY VS. BOX-AND-1

Hubie Brown, Head Coach,
Memphis Grizzlies, Memphis, Tenn.

DIAGRAM 1: For this diagram, S will be your star player. W should be a good shooter and P2 will be the better scorer of the two post players.

1 enters the ball by dribbling to the middle.

DIAGRAM 2: S should run all over the court, using curls, cuts and various moves to take his or her defender all over the floor.

DIAGRAM 3: 1 passes to W, while P1 sets a screen on P2's defender. S continues to try to shake his or her defender.

DIAGRAM 4: P2 pops out to the wing area, while W quickly ball reverses to 1 who looks to P2 for a quick 10- to 12-foot jump-shot.

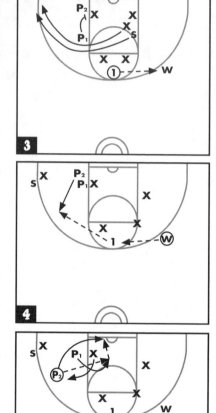

DIAGRAM 5: If the low defender fights through P1's screen by coming over the top, then P1 and P2 should run a quick give-and-go play toward the basket.

"WING AWAY" (SET PLAY VS. ZONE)

Doug Hughes, Basketball Coach,
Saint Henry, Ohio

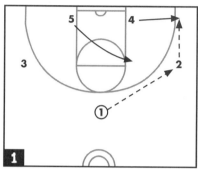

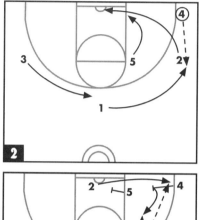

DIAGRAM 1: 1 is on top and has the ball, while 2 and 3 line up wide on the wings. 5 and 4 set up in the low post on each side. 1 passes to 2, while 5 cuts up to the ball-side elbow. 4 pops to the ball-side corner and receives a pass from 2.

DIAGRAM 2: 2 cuts to the basket and goes all the way under the basket. 1 replaces 2 at the ball-side wing, while 3 replaces 1 on top. 5 rolls down to the ball-side low block.

4 looks to hit 2 cutting through the lane for a quick layup. If that pass isn't there, then 4 kicks the ball back out to 1 on the wing.

DIAGRAM 3: 1 must draw the defense out by taking two or three hard dribbles toward 3 on top. 5 and 4 set a double screen for 2 who rolls back out to the ball-side corner behind the 3-point line. After setting the screen, 4 rolls to the basket. 1 can hit 2 in the corner for a quick 3-pointer or hit 4 rolling off the screen for a short jump shot.

UNDERNEATH INBOUNDS PLAY (VS. ZONE)

Michael Burris,
Olney Central College,
Olney, Ill.

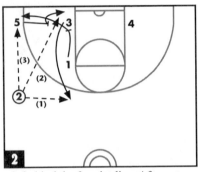

DIAGRAM 1: This play is run from a box-set formation with a post player on each block and your guards at the elbows. 5 pops to the ball-side corner and receives a pass from 3. 2 comes off 1's screen and goes behind the 3-point line on the ball side. 5 swings the ball to 2.

DIAGRAM 2: 1 sets a downscreen for 3 who breaks out to the top of the circle behind the 3-point line. After setting the screen, 1 flashes to the ball-side corner off a screen set by 5. If the defender stays in, then 1 will be open. If the defender comes out to guard 1, then 5 will be free to slip toward the basket and receive a pass for a post-up opportunity. 2 has three passing options: **1.** A pass to 3 for a 3-pointer. **2.** 5 on a roll toward the basket. **3.** 1 in the corner for a 3-point shot.

SET PLAY VS. 2-3 ZONE

Dale Herl,
Lyons, Kan.

DIAGRAM 1: 4 must line up inside the zone on the baseline. 5 lines up between the two defenders at the top of the zone. 1 passes to 3. 1 cuts down the lane toward the basket and fades to the weak-side baseline corner away from the pass.

DIAGRAM 2: 5 pops out to the top. 3 reverses the ball to 5. 4 moves to the outer side of the zone near the baseline.

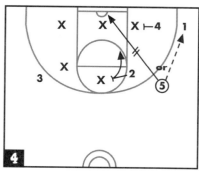

DIAGRAM 3: 2 sets an on-ball screen for 5. 4 screens the bottom of the zone. 5 dribbles to the wing.

DIAGRAM 4: 5 comes off the screen for the shot or 1 will receive the pass and shoot a 3-pointer. After setting the screen, 2 rolls toward the basket.

SET PLAY VS. ZONE

Alan McAughtry,
Melbourne, Australia

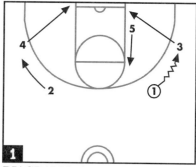

DIAGRAM 1: 1 enters the ball by dribbling to the wing. 5 cuts to the high post. 3 cuts to the low post. 4 cuts to the low post below the backboard on the weak side. 2 steps to the weak-side free-throw line extended.

DIAGRAM 2: 5 downscreens for 4 and 4 breaks to the high post. 3 headhunts 5's defender. 4 goes to the high post looking to receive the pass from 1. 2 should be spotting up in case the nearest defender helps to the ball side.

"CLEVELAND" VS. SOFT 1-2-2 OR 2-3 ZONE

Jeff Tarkowski,
Racine St. Catherine's High School,
Racine, Wis.

This is a very simple play vs. a 2-3 or a soft 1-2-2 zone. For this play to work, your point guard must be tough with the ball and have good court vision.

You'll need one good shooter, a point guard and three other players to work the boards and set picks. The player with the hot hand is shooting and everyone else is working to get that player the ball or grab the offensive rebound.

DIAGRAM 1: This is the initial set. 4 and 5 set up a double stack in the low post. 3 lines up on the opposite low block and 2 floats in the wing area.

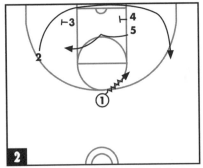

DIAGRAM 2: 1 drives at the defensive guard and takes the defender

toward the side of the floor with the stack. 5 flashes into the lane and posts up for a one-count. 2 cuts to the basket using staggered screens set by 3 and 4 along the baseline.

DIAGRAM 3: 1 looks for 2 open on the wing for the 3-pointer or for 5 posting in the lane for the one-count. 1 must read the defensive forward. If the forward stays home, 2 will have an open shot, but if the defender jumps out, then 4 will be open in the low-post block area.

If nothing opens up, 2 cuts back to the other side using the staggered screens by 3 and 4 along the baseline, with 5 flashing back into the lane.

1 breaks down the defender by using the dribble and heads toward the other side of the floor looking for an open player.

DIAGRAM 4: This is a variation of the play if the defense starts making adjustments. 1 takes the defender toward the right side of the floor. This time, 2 uses the first screen by 3 and curls up through the lane to the top of the key. 5 flashes into the lane for a

one-count and then pops out to the offside elbow.

DIAGRAM 5: On any shot by 2, 1 gets back down court to prevent any possible transition breaks. 4, 5 and 3 form a rebounding triangle and intensely box out in order to grab the offensive board.

SPREAD UNDERNEATH INBOUND VS. ZONE

Lason Perkins, Former Coach,
Cary High School,
Cary, N.C.

DIAGRAM 1: 1 passes to 2 or 3. 5 looks to flash to the ball and seal the middle defender. 4 serves as a safety.

DIAGRAM 2: 1 inbounds to 2. 2 looks to 5 in the post. If 5 is not open, 2 brings the ball up to the top. 4 dives into the lane and 1 steps inbounds behind 2.

DIAGRAM 3: 2 passes back to 1. 4 cuts to the short corner to overload the zone.

ZONE OFFENSE VS. 2-MAN FRONTS

Keith Siefkes,
Beth Eden Baptist School,
Denver, Colo.

This offense is most effective against a 2-man front zone or a box-and-1 defense.

DIAGRAM 1: For this offense, 4 should be your best shooter and is initially set up in the low post. 1 has the ball at the top, while 5 is at the free-throw line. 2 and 3 line up wide in each wing area behind the 3-point line.

DIAGRAM 2: 1 dribbles away from 4's side of the floor and to the right wing area to start the action. As 1 dribbles toward 2, 2 sets a baseline screen for 4.

After setting the screen, 2 releases to the top of the key for ball reversal. 5 rolls toward the ball to the mid-post area and 3 drops on the weak side for rebounding.

1 can pass to 4 off the screen to 2 after the screen in the low post or 5 at the mid-post.

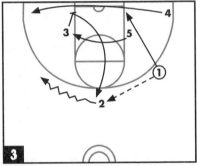

DIAGRAM 3: For ball reversal, 1 passes to 2. 2 dribbles to the opposite wing as 3 moves to screen for 4. 5 follows the ball to the strong-side mid-post and 1 drops for weak-side rebounding. After the screen, 3 releases to the top for ball reversal.

DIAGRAM 4: We use this pattern for a quicker ball reversal. The play begins the same, with 1 dribbling to the wing.

After 2 sets the baseline screen for 4, 2 releases to the opposite wing. 5 steps out for ball reversal.

DIAGRAM 5: The reversal pass goes from 1 to 5 to 2.

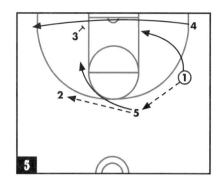

"THREE LOW" (VS. ZONE)

Alan McAughtry,
Melbourne, Australia

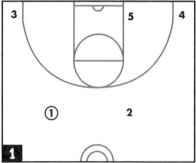

DIAGRAM 1: Start with 3, 5 and 4 positioned low and 1 and 2 set up high. 1 has the ball.

DIAGRAM 2: 1 dribbles to the weak side and passes to 3 in the corner. 5 cuts across the lane and up to the weak-side elbow. 2 breaks to the opposite wing area.

DIAGRAM 3: As 5 cuts high, 4 sneaks in low behind the zone and posts up as close to the basket as he or she can. 3 can throw to 4 or pass to 5 at the elbow when the defense closes in on 4 as he or she tries to post up.

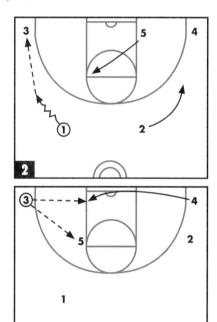

POST-UP PLAY VS. TRIANGLE-AND-2 ZONE

Hubie Brown, Head Coach,
Memphis Grizzlies,
Memphis, Tenn.

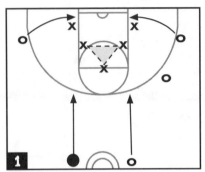

DIAGRAM 1: Have your two guards come down at the top and attack the triangle at the lane-line extended. The ball handler is on the left. Your two post players break from behind the 3-point line on each side and establish position behind the bottom two zone defenders.

DIAGRAM 2: 1 takes a few hard dribbles back up toward the top of the key. Note how compact the defense currently is and that there are now four defenders under the dotted line!

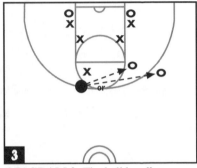

DIAGRAM 3: The ball handler throws a pass to the weak side to either the player at the elbow (if the top defender has slid over to attack the ball handler) or the far wing player.

DIAGRAM 4: The player who receives the pass immediately "sells" shooting a jump shot, causing the defender on his or her side to break up and close out. The player with the ball quickly feeds the post player on the ball-side low block.

DIAGRAM 5: You now have a 1-on-1 situation in the post and a good opportunity for that player to get off a high-percentage shot.

This play can easily be run from the other side with ball entry on the opposite side.

THUMBS-UP (VS. 1-2-2)

Steve Mergelsberg, Assistant Coach,
Rutgers University — Newark,
Newark, N.J.

DIAGRAM 1: 1 makes a dribble entry to the right side. As he or she dribbles past the free-throw line extended, 3 sets a back screen for 5 (3's defender will often chase him or her up the lane). 5 comes off the screen and rolls to the basket, looking for a pass from 1 for a quick layup. If 5 doesn't get the pass, then he or she posts up on the ball-side low block.

On the opposite side, 2 and 4 exchange positions to help create movement. If 5 gets a pass from 1 on the ball side, 4's defender often slides over to provide defensive help. This could create an opening for 5 to dish to 4 cutting to the hoop.

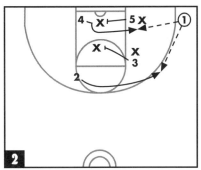

DIAGRAM 2: If there is nothing on the roll or quick post-up, then 5 turns and screens away for 4, who breaks to the ball-side low block.

Meanwhile, 3 sets a screen in the lane on the defender closest to 2, who uses the screen and sprints toward the ball side. 1 can either hit 4 for a post-up shot down low or pass to 2 for a short jump shot at the elbow.

SET PLAY VS. 2-3 ZONE

Hubie Brown, Head Coach,
Memphis Grizzlies, Memphis, Tenn.

DIAGRAM 1: Player 1 dribbles to the right side and passes to 3. After the zone defenders come out to guard 3, 3 passes back to 1.

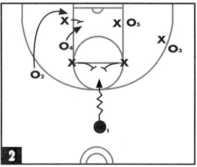

DIAGRAM 2: 1 dribbles toward the middle of the zone, drawing the top defenders together. 4 cuts into the lane, drawing the left-baseline defender to the middle. As that defender cuts to the middle, 2 cuts behind him or her.

DIAGRAM 3: 3 cuts into the lane and the wing defender will follow to the middle. 1 fakes a pass to either 4 or 3 in the middle. As the fake is going on, 2 breaks back out to the wing area.

DIAGRAM 4: The zone is now compact and 1 passes to 2 on the wing for an easy 5-, 10- or 15-foot jump shot.

"Great teams have guards that can penetrate, break down the defense and move the ball."

—*Kevin McHale*

Chapter 8

3-POINT PLAYS

"HOOSIER" FOR 3-POINTS

Eddie Sutton, Head Mens Coach,
Oklahoma State University,
Stillwater, Okla.

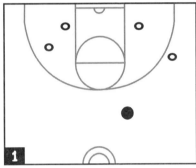

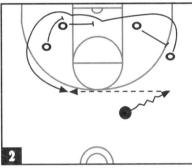

DIAGRAM 1: The player you want shooting the 3-pointer is set up in the right-wing area. Your two best rebounders should be set up on the left-hand side.

DIAGRAM 2: The ball handler dribbles to the right side of the floor. The low-block player on the right side pops up and sets a screen for the wing player. The player on the right wing uses the screen and breaks toward the bas-ket. The player continues to cut along the baseline and comes off the screens and pops behind the 3-point line.

The ball handler throws a skip pass to the player coming off the double screen and shoots a 3-pointer. The two lowest screeners must crash the boards.

If any defender switches or helps, the nearest screener steps back and he or she will be wide open for a shot.

> *"Basketball is a game that's easy*
> *to play and difficult to master."*
>
> —*James Naismith*

DOUBLE-SCREEN SPECIAL FOR 3-POINTS

Chris Croft, Head Mens Coach,
Martin Methodist College, Pulaski, Tenn.

DIAGRAM 1: In the initial set, 4 and 5 line up at the weak-side elbow. 1 has the ball on the right side. 2 sets a screen for 3 who breaks along the baseline to the opposite side.

DIAGRAM 3: 1 sets a downscreen for 3. 3 comes off the screen and pops behind the 3-point line. 2 passes to 3. 4 and 5 remain on the opposite block.

DIAGRAM 2: 4 and 5 set a double screen for 2 who pops to the top. 1 dribbles a few steps left and delivers the pass to 2. 3 remains near the baseline on the weak side.

DIAGRAM 4: 1 breaks hard along the baseline and comes off a double screen set by 4 and 5. 3 passes to 2 who quickly skip passes to 1 coming off the double screen. 1 shoots a 3-pointer.

"The harder you prepare, the luckier you get."

—Michael Jordan

SIDE OUT-OF-BOUNDS FOR 3-POINTER

Keith Cooper, Assistant Mens Coach,
Central Washington University,
Ellensburg, Wash.

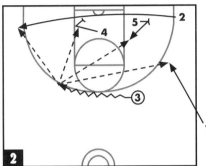

DIAGRAM 1: 3 and 5 set baseline screens for 2, who cuts up then uses the screens and breaks along the baseline to the ball-side corner. 4 downscreens for 3. 1 looks for 2 or 3 coming off the screens for a 3-point shot.

DIAGRAM 2: If there's no immediate shot, then 1 passes in to 3 who dribbles hard and attacks the opposite side of the floor. 2 comes back to the other side using baseline screens by 4 and 5. After setting the screens, 4 seals his or her defender in the post and 5 flashes to the weak-side mid-post area.

3 looks to hit 2 for a 3-pointer, 4 in the lane, 5 on the weak-side mid-post or throws a return pass to 1 stepping inbound for a quick 3-point shot.

"BUCKET" FOR 3-POINT SHOT

Vonn Read, Advance Scout,
Orlando Magic,
Orlando, Fla.

DIAGRAM 1: 1 passes to 3, while 2 breaks up and sets a screen for 4 cutting to the basket on the weak side. 3 dribbles hard into the corner to draw the defense. As 3 is dribbling, 1 and 5 set a double screen for 2, who uses the screens and cuts around the top of the key, breaking behind the 3-point line on the ball side. 3 throws a quick pass to 2 for the 3-point shot.

INBOUND PASS FOR 3-POINTER

Mack McCarthy, Former Mens Head Coach,
Virginia Commonwealth University,
Richmond Va.

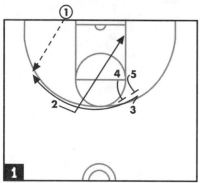

DIAGRAM 1: 1 takes the ball out. 2 cuts to the opposite block. 4 and 5 set a staggered screen for 3. 3 cuts to the strong side wing. 1 passes to 3.

DIAGRAM 2: 3 looks for the shot first. If there is no shot available, 4 and 5 screen down for 2. 2 pops out to the top off the double screen. 3 takes one or two hard dribbles and passes to 2. If 2 is covered, 3 may look back to 1, who has stepped back in bounds.

"L.A." SET PLAY FOR 3-POINT SHOT (VS. MAN)

Rhonda Farney, Head Girls Coach,
And Kellye Richardson, Assistant Girls Coach,
Georgetown High School,
Georgetown, Texas

DIAGRAM 1: 1 has the ball on the right side and passes to 2 breaking up from the right low block. 3 cuts down

and replaces 2 on the ball-side low block, while 4 pops up from the left low block to the top. 5 stays at the foul line.

After making the pass to 2, 1 cuts through to the weak-side low block.
DIAGRAM 2: 1 breaks from the weak-side low block to the weak-side wing area. 2 passes to 4 and 4 swings the ball quickly over to 1. After making the pass, 2 cuts to the basket, comes off a screen set by 3 and breaks through to the opposite low post.
DIAGRAM 3: 1 fakes a pass to 2 in

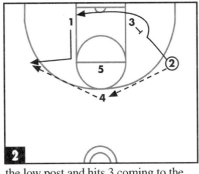

the low post and hits 3 coming to the top off a set of staggered screens from

4 and 5. 3 catches the pass, squares up and shoots a quick 3-pointer.

HALF-COURT SET FOR 3-POINT SHOT

Keith Cooper, Assistant Mens Coach,
Central Washington University,
Ellensburg, Wash.

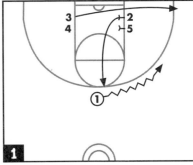

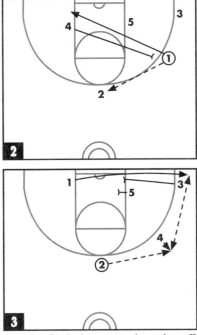

DIAGRAM 1: 1 dribbles to the right wing area. 2 and 5 set a double screen for 3 who cuts to the corner. After setting the screen, 2 loops to the top of the key. 4 and 5 remain in the post.

DIAGRAM 2: 1 passes to 2. 4 breaks up and sets a diagonal back pick for 1, who cuts hard to the left low block. 5 remains on the block, while 3 stays behind the 3-point line.

DIAGRAM 3: 4 steps out after setting the back pick and receives a pass from 2. 3 and 5 set a double screen on the baseline for 1. 4 passes to 1 coming off the baseline double screen. 1 shoots a 3-pointer.

"KENTUCKY" FOR 3-POINTS

Chris Kusnerick, Head Boys Coach,
St. Anthony High School,
Effingham, Ill.

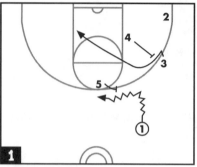

DIAGRAM 1: 1 begins the play by executing a dribble-entry to the right side of the floor. 5 sets a screen for 1, who uses the screen, keeps the dribble alive and centers the ball at the top of the key. 4 breaks to the wing and sets an upscreen for 3, who V-cuts and breaks to the opposite low block.

DIAGRAM 2: 4 and 5 set staggered downscreens for 2 on the weak side. 2 uses the screens and pops to the top of the key behind the 3-point line. 1 passes to 2 for a quick 3-pointer.

"TRIPLE"

Greg Fortner, Head Girls Coach,
Fox High School,
Arnold, Mo.

We have run this play successfully over the years from a 1-2-2 offensive set. You can run it strictly for a 3-point shot or it can also get you a long-range 2-pointer.

DIAGRAM 1: 1 has the ball on top and dribbles right, then cuts back to the left. 2 cuts along the baseline and comes off a triple screen set by 4, 5 and 3. 1 hits 2 in the corner for a 3-pointer.

DIAGRAM 2: If 2 doesn't get a clean look at a 3-point shot, 1 breaks down and sets a screen for 3 who curls

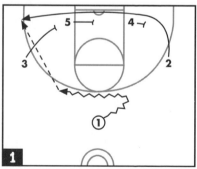

around the screen and pops to the ball-side wing area.

After setting the screen, 1 drops down and sets the first of another triple screen for 2. 2 passes to 3 on the wing and uses the triple screen set by 1, 5 and 4 to run the baseline and head to the weak-side corner.

3 dribbles hard to the right and hits 2 coming off the baseline triple screen for a 3-point shot.

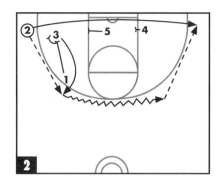

3-POINT SPECIAL FOR POINT GUARD

Randy Brown, Former Assistant Coach,
Iowa State University,
Ames, Iowa

DIAGRAM 1: 4 and 5 set down-screens for 2 and 3. 1 passes to 2. After the pass, 1 helps screen for 3.

DIAGRAM 2: 5 sets a cross screen for 4 cutting to the ball-side block. After 4 has cleared the screen, 5 comes to the top of the key. 2 passes to 5.

DIAGRAM 3: As soon as 5 catches the pass, 4 and 2 set staggered screens for 1 clearing for an open 3-point shot.

QUICK "3" WITH OPTIONS

Vinod Vachani, Head Girls Coach,
Welham Girls' High School
Dehra Dun, India

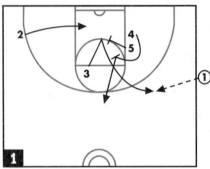 

DIAGRAM 1: 4 and 5 set a screen for 3. 1 passes the ball to 3 for a quick-hitting 3-point shot. After setting the screen, 4 rolls out to the top and becomes a safety release.

DIAGRAM 2: Option. 3 sets a down-screen for 2 and rolls out. 1 inbounds the ball to 2. 5 flashes the high post, 4 sets a back screen for 1. 2 can either shoot the three or pass (lob) to 1 cutting to the basket.

"TOP" FOR 3-POINTER

Bill Agronin, Head Womens Coach,
Niagara University,
Niagara, N.Y.

DIAGRAM 1: 4 breaks to the wing and receives a pass from 1. 1 cuts toward the baseline along the outside of the lane on the ball side.
DIAGRAM 2: 4 passes to 5 and quickly sets a screen for 3 who breaks behind the ball-side 3-point line. 5 sets a screen for 1 who pops to the ball-side 3-point area. 3 can either shoot a 3-pointer or pass to 1 for the shot.

SET PLAY FOR 3-POINTS

Chad Even, Basketball Coach,
Napoleon High School,
Napoleon, N.D.

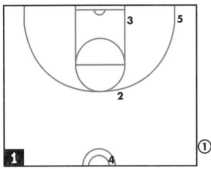

DIAGRAM 1: 1 inbounds the ball, while 4 lines up at half court and 5 is in the strong-side corner. 3 lines up on the strong-side low post and 2 is on top behind the 3-point line at the lane-line extended.

2 and 3 can flip positions to get the better 3-point shooter out on top.

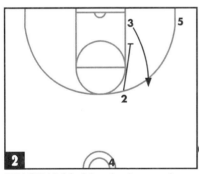

DIAGRAM 2: 2 breaks down and sets a screen for 3 who comes off the screen and rolls toward the ball side behind the 3-point line.

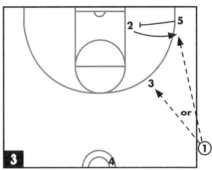

DIAGRAM 3: 5 locates 2's defender and screens-in. 2 uses the screen and rolls to the strong side behind the 3-point line. 1 looks for either 2 or 3 for an open 3-pointer.

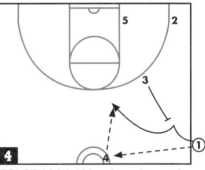

DIAGRAM 4: If 2 or 3 aren't open for the 3-point look, 1 throws to 4 as a safety. On the inbound pass to 4, 3 steps up and sets a back screen on 1's defender.

4 looks to hit 1 rolling off the screen for an open 3-point play. If the defenders get caught up on the 3-to-1 screen-switch, then 3 may come open and 4 can look to hit 3 for a 3-point shot.

1-4 SET PLAY FOR 3-POINTER

Vonn Read, Advanced Scout
Orlando Magic,
Orlando, Fla.

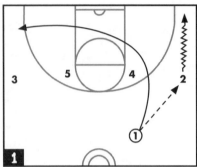

DIAGRAM 1: Run from a 1-4 set. 1 passes to 2 and cuts toward the basket, breaking all the way through to the off-side 3-point corner. 2 dribbles into the baseline corner.

DIAGRAM 2: 5 and 4 set a staggered screen for 3 who comes across the top to receive a pass from 2. After receiving the pass from 2, 3 squares up and shoots the 3-pointer.

3-POINTER FROM A 1-4 HIGH SET

Bill Agronin, Head Womens Coach,
Niagara University,
Niagara, N.Y.

DIAGRAM 1: 1 dribbles to the right and throws a quick pass to 4 breaking up from the weak-side elbow to the top. After making the pass, 5 pops up and 2 slides over to set a double screen for 1 fading into the opposite corner.

DIAGRAM 2: 4 passes over the top and hits 1 for a 3-point shot. 2 steps back behind the 3-point line on the perimeter and if the defenses collapses down on 1, 1 can pass to 2 for a 3-pointer. 3 crashes the boards from the weak side.

QUICK HITTER FOR THREE (VS. MAN)

Alan McAughtry,
Melbourne, Australia

DIAGRAM 1: Four players line up flat along the baseline. 1 signals and the ball-side post player (5) steps up to the elbow to set up in the high-post.

DIAGRAM 3: As 4 receives the pass from 1, 2 steps-out wide and 1 cuts hard off the screen by 5 and fills 2's position on the low block.

DIAGRAM 2: 4 steps up high to receive the pass from 1. At the same time, 3 makes a cut to the same position as 4 on the opposite side.

DIAGRAM 4: 4 passes to 2 and sets a double screen with 5. 3 comes hard over the top to receive the pass from 2 for the 3-point shot. *Note:* 3 can alternate this cut with a fake and backdoor cut.

> *"Obviously, there have been times when I've failed. But there have never been times when I thought I would fail."*
>
> —Michael Jordan

Chapter 9

SPECIALS, SITUATIONAL PLAYS

SET PLAY VS. AN OVERPLAYING DEFENSE

Mitch Mitchell,
Copiah Academy,
Gallman, Miss.

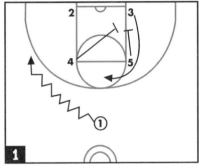

DIAGRAM 1: We use this play when teams are really overplaying the passing lanes on our best player. 1 dribbles to the free-throw line extended. 4 and 5 set a double screen for 3.

DIAGRAM 2: On the ball reversal to 3, 1 cuts through the lane to run off a double screen from 4 and 5.

DIAGRAM 3: As 1 goes by 2, 2 pops to the wing and makes a hard back cut.

DIAGRAM 4: If 2 isn't open on the backdoor cut, 1 becomes the second option curling off the double screen. 2 is the third option, continuing through the lane and off the double screen from 4 and 5 for the jumper.

POST ISOLATION "ISO"

Brent Brannon, Assistant Boys Coach,
Calhoun High School,
Calhoun, Ga.

This set play is designed to isolate a post player in the low block or a guard or small forward who has the ability to post up.

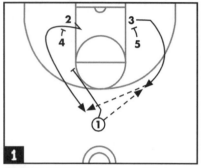

DIAGRAM 1: Out of a modified stack set, 4 and 5 screen down for 2 and 3. 1 passes to 3. After making the pass, 1 downscreens for 2, who comes off the staggered screens by 4 and 1 and looks for a pass from 3.

If 2 has a clean look, he or she should take the shot. If not, he or she should make a return pass to 3.

DIAGRAM 2: If no shot is taken by 2, then 1 should pop back out. 3 passes to 2 who reverses the ball to 1. 4 and 5 remain in post-up position on opposite blocks.

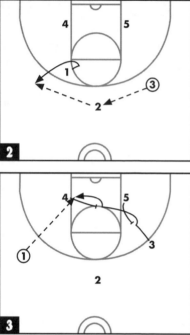

DIAGRAM 3: As the ball is in the air on the pass from 2 to 1, 5 steps up and sets a back screen on 3's defender. 4 also back screens for 3 to help isolate him or her on the ball-side low block. 1 enters the ball in to 3 who's coming off 4's screen. 3 works for the shot on a post-up isolation move.

"More depth, more options and great competition in practice — these things make you a better team."

—*Mike Krzyzewski*

TEMPO-SETTING JUMP-BALL PLAY

DuWayne Krause,
Magic Valley Christian School,
Twin Falls, Idaho

We've used the following jump-ball play with a great deal of success. It only takes 5 minutes to teach, maintains safe defensive coverage and puts your team in "attack mode" right from the opening toss of the ball. If we score off this play, we'll immediately press in an attempt to rattle the opponent.

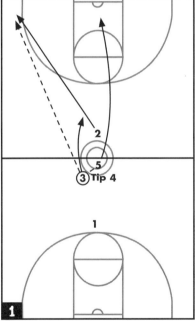

DIAGRAM 1: Option A. 5 tips the ball to 3, while 2 breaks to the left corner. 5 streaks straight to the basket while 3 passes to 2 downcourt. 3 sprints to the ball-side perimeter.

The two main options for 2 are to shoot a quick 3-pointer or hit 5 for a layup. 2 can also look to hit 3 as a trailer for a spot-up jumper.

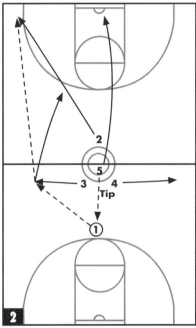

DIAGRAM 2: Option B. If the tip goes to 1, the play is the same, except that 3 and 4 flare to each sideline as 1 gets the ball. 1 passes to 3, while 2 breaks to the left corner. 5 streaks straight to the basket while 3 passes to 2 downcourt. 3 sprints to the ball-side perimeter.

The two main options are still the same: 2 for a quick 3-pointer or 5 for a layup. 2 also looks to hit 3 as a trailer for a spot-up jumper.

"SAFETY" FULL-COURT INBOUNDS

Pat Sullivan, Head Mens Coach,
University Of St. Francis,
Joliet, Ill.

DIAGRAM 1: 1 takes the ball out, while the rest of the team lines up in a 4-player stack next to the foul line on the ball-side, starting at the mid-post area.

On the "Break!" call initiated by 1, 5 sets a screen for 2, who makes a V-cut and comes hard to the ball. 4 pops to the ball-side corner and 3 breaks to the weak-side corner. After setting the screen for 2, 5 releases deep and sprints long.

1 looks to hit 5 with a deep baseball pass first (A), then looks to pass to 2 (B) or 3 (C). If the pass goes to 2 or 3, they must immediately pass back to 1 who leads the offensive attack downcourt.

"CURL" QUICK-HITTING PLAY TO END A QUARTER

Brad McGhee, Head Boys Coach,
Liberty High School,
Mountain View, Mo.

DIAGRAM 1: 1 has the ball up top, while 3 lines up on the ball-side elbow. 4, 5, and 2 form a stack on the weak-side low block. 3 pops up and sets a screen for 1.

DIAGRAM 2: 1 uses 3's screen and dribbles right. After setting the screen, 3 rolls back toward the basket and looks for the pass from 1 on the pick-and-roll action for a score. 2 pops from the bottom of the triple stack to the top of the key.

DIAGRAM 3: If the pick-and-roll option to 3 isn't there, 3 continues his or her cut all the way to basket and comes off a double screen set by 4 and

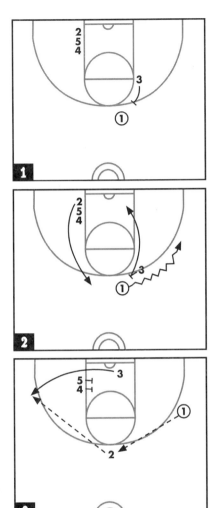

DIAGRAM 4: If 3 isn't open coming off the double screen, 2 looks to hit 5 curling around a screen set by 4 and rolling to the basket for a post-up opportunity.

DIAGRAM 5: Another option is to have 1 V-cut after the making the pass to 2 and cut to the basket. 2 would fake a reversal pass to 3 on the overload side and hit 1 for a layup on the backside.

5 and fades into the weak-side corner.

1 passes to 2, who looks to quickly swing the ball to 3 in the corner for a 3-point shot.

> *"The great teams learn how to win night after night, week after week, season after season, with no letup."*
>
> —*Don Nelson*

"GOING LONG"

Ron Jirsa, Assistant Mens Coach,
Clemson University,
Clemson, S.C.

Here are two full court plays for two different situations both run from the same set. These plays will prepare your team for two different full-court situations. By using the same set your team will be difficult to scout.

to the top of the key. The three perimeter players start toward the passer, then cut back toward the basket. The receiver (5) either tips the pass to a perimeter player for the shot or catches and shoots for the basket.

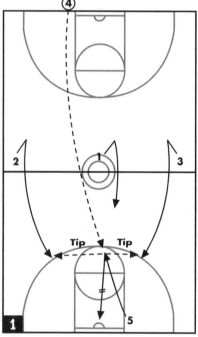

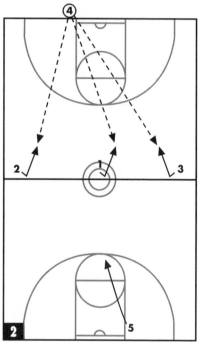

DIAGRAM 1: "Home Run." This is a full-court play for a 2- or 3-point basket. It's good for situations when a long pass is necessary because there's not enough time left to advance the ball up the court on the dribble. The best passer throws a timing pass to an athletic receiver cutting from the block

DIAGRAM 2: "Triple." This play is designed to advance the ball to half court for a time-out.

All three players take two full steps toward their basket and then break toward the ball. The pass must be in the air as the player is breaking back toward the ball to receive it.

PLAY TO END A QUARTER

Andy Landers, Head Womens Coach,
University of Georgia,
Athens, Ga.

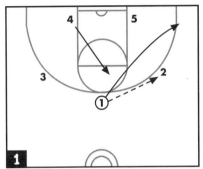

DIAGRAM 1: This is a great scoring play to use at the end of a quarter or half. Out of the the initial set, 1 handles the ball at the top of the key. 4 flashes to the free-throw line. 1 passes to 2 and cuts to the ball-side corner.

DIAGRAM 3: 5 sets a screen for 1 on the weak side. It's important that 1 take his or her time and slowly walk toward the screen. 1 explodes off the screen from 5 and bursts to the top of the key. 3 passes to 1 who looks for a quick shot.

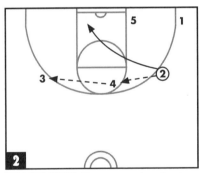

DIAGRAM 2: 2 passes to 4 and cuts to the basket. 4 swings the ball to 3. 2 settles in on the ball-side block.

DIAGRAM 4: If 1 doesn't have a shot, 4 and 5 should break to the ball-side block and set a double screen for 2. 2 comes off the screens and breaks up behind the weak-side 3-point line. 1 hits 2 for a quick 3-pointer.

A GOOD BUT SIMPLE TAP PLAY

A.J. Giovannangeli,
Conant High School,
Jaffrey, N.H.

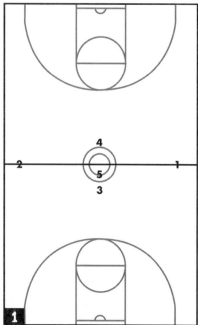

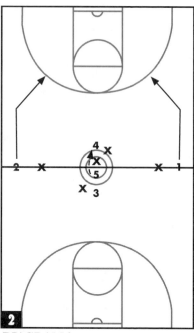

DIAGRAM 1: This play is perfect when you're fortunate enough to have a center who can win control of the jump ball. Your guards (1 and 2) should be positioned wide of the circle near the sideline. 3 is in the backcourt and 4 is in the front court.

DIAGRAM 2: As the jump pass is thrown in the air, 2 and 1 break hard down court, both breaking toward the basket around the top of the 3-point circle. 5 taps the jump to 4.

> *"The team itself must be*
> *the leader of the team."*
>
> —Phil Jackson

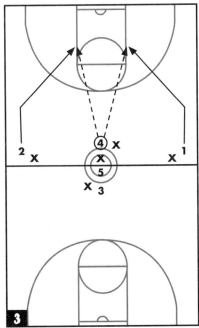

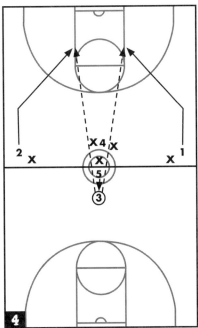

DIAGRAM 3: 4 quickly turns, eyes the basket and fires a pass to either 2 or 1 streaking down court for an easy layup. If the layup is not there, have your players go immediately into your fast-break offense.

DIAGRAM 4: If the opponent has this play scouted out and double-teams 4, then 5 should tip the jump pass to 3 in the back court. 3 fires the pass to either 1 or 2 streaking down court for a layup.

END-OF-QUARTER, END-OF-HALF SPECIAL

Vonn Read, Advance Scout,
Orlando Magic, NBA,
Orlando, Fla.

DIAGRAM 1: 1 inbounds the ball from side court, while 4 and 5 are positioned in a stack in the lane just in front of the basket. 3 lines up near 1 at the top and 2 lines up in the opposite corner.

On the action initiated by 1, 2 breaks across the baseline and to the ball-side corner. 4 breaks up and sets a screen for 3 who busts to the opposite wing area behind the 3-point line. As 4 makes his or her break to set the screen, 5 may be left open for an easy entry pass in the

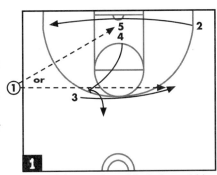

post. If the pass in to 5 isn't there, 1 hits 3 cross-court for a 3-pointer.